Building Basic Skills in Science

Building Basic Skills in Science

Contemporary Books, Inc.
Chicago

Library of Congress Cataloging in Publication Data
Main entry under title:

Building basic skills in science.

1. Science—Examinations, questions, etc.
I. Contemporary Books, inc.
Q182.B84   507'.6   81-851
ISBN 0-8092-5973-7 (pbk.)   AACR2

Published by Contemporary Books, Inc.
180 North Michigan Avenue, Chicago, Illinois 60601
Manufactured in the United States of America
Library of Congress Catalog Card Number: 81-851
International Standard Book Number: 0-8092-5973-7

Published simultaneously in Canada by
Beaverbooks, Ltd.
150 Lesmill Road
Don Mills, Ontario M3B 2T5
Canada

ACKNOWLEDGMENTS

The thoughtful efforts of a great many people went into the preparation of Contemporary Books' *Building Basic Skills* series. We gratefully acknowledge their contributions and continued involvement in Adult Education.

Adult Education Division

Lillian J. Fleming, Editorial Director
Barbara Drazin, Editor
Wendy Harris, Marketing Services Coordinator

Production Department

Deborah Eisel, Production Editor

Reading and Readability Editors

Jane L. Evanson   Deborah Nathan
Helen B. Ward   Jane Friedland
Norma Libman   Donna Wynbrandt

Authors and Contributors

Writing: Rob Sax

Social Studies: Robert Schambier
    Carol Hagel
    Phil Smolik
    Jack Lesar
    Nora Ishibashi
    Helen T. Bryant
    Jo Ann Kawell
    Deborah Brewster
    Mary E. Bromage
    Sheldon B. Silver
    Patricia Miripol

Science: Ronald LeMay
    Cynthia Talbert
    Jeffrey Miripol
    John Gloor
    William Collien
    Charles Nissim-Sabat

Reading: Timothy A. Foote
    Raymond Traynor
    Pamela D. Drell (Editor)

Mathematics: Jerry Howett

Project Assistance
    Sara Plath

Graphic Art: Louise Hodges
Cover Design: Jeff Barnes

CONTENTS

TO THE LEARNER

Building Basic Skills in Science from Contemporary Books is planned with you the learner in mind. Your work in this book will start to build your science knowledge while it gives you practice building your reading skills.

HOW TO GET THE MOST FROM THIS BOOK

TAKE THE
PRE-TEST

A good way to start your work in *Building Basic Skills in Science* is to take the **Pre-Test.** The 25 questions will give you a good idea of your strengths before you start to work. The reading passages and questions on the Pre-Test will also give you a feel for what's coming in the book.

The Pre-Test is made up of science reading passages followed by reading skill questions. There are also questions that come from cartoons, graphs or charts. Finally, we have also put in some science questions that stand alone. These will tell what you already know about some science topics. In working all the questions, remember that there is no time limit. You may take as much time as you need. Remember that the Pre-Test is meant to be a way to show where your skills are *before* you begin building them. Afterwards, the Post-Test will show how much your work has paid off.

CHECK YOUR
PRE-TEST
ANSWERS

RECORD YOUR
SCORE

You will be able to check your work using the **Answers and Explanations** that follow the Pre-Test. The reading and science skills needed for each question are shown here too. Finally, remember to record your score on the **Pre-Test Skill Record** (page 14).

Four units of science make up this skill-building book. They are:

Biology—the study of all living things—plants and animals

Earth Science—the study of everything about our planet, from rocks and rivers to land and sky

Chemistry—the study of matter and all the changes that happen to substances

Physics—the study of how matter and energy work—light, sound, heat and electricity

WORK THROUGH THE FOUR SCIENCE UNITS

Each science unit is made up of reading passages that are written about many different science topics. Working through the passages will build both your science reading skills and your science knowledge.

A list of **Key Words** comes before each science reading passage. These words give you an idea of what the passage is about. They are used in the passage along with other words that may be new to you.

STUDY THE KEY WORDS

We have listed many of these words (and all of the Key Words) in the helpful Glossary at the end of the book. The **Glossary** gives the meanings of words and is a good tool for reviewing what you learn from the passages.

USE THE GLOSSARY

Five reading skill questions follow each science passage. These questions have been written to build your reading skills. They follow this plan:

First Reading Skill Question	Finding the main idea of the passage
Second Reading Skill Question	Recalling a supporting detail
Third Reading Skill Question Fourth Reading Skill Question	Recalling a supporting detail OR Seeing relationships cause and effect comparison and contrast
Fifth Reading Skill Question	Drawing a conclusion from the passage

ANSWER THE READING SKILL QUESTIONS

Each kind of reading skill question asks you to use a different kind of thinking to answer the question. We should tell you more about the skills:

MAIN IDEA

The main idea is what the passage is about. It is made up of a topic and what is then said about the topic. It is the important point that the writer wants the reader to understand. Most of the facts, or details, in the passage relate to the main idea. The main idea of a science reading passage is often found near the beginning. The main idea also may be repeated at the end of the passage.

DETAILS

Details, or facts, support the main idea. They add to it and give it more meaning. You have to pay attention to details, even small ones. They do count.

RELATIONSHIP

Readers have to judge the connections between things. There are many kinds of relationships, or connections, in nature. One is the cause and effect relationship. If you hit a ball with a bat, hitting the ball is the physical cause that makes the ball fly through the air. A ball flying through the air is an effect of hitting the ball with a bat.

Comparison and contrast is another kind of connection that a reader has to make. This relationship is between two things which are not normally connected. Comparison means looking at one thing next to another thing and describing how they're alike. You can compare an orange to an apple. They are both fruits. Both can be eaten. Contrast means seeing how those things are different. How is a star different from a planet? How is a river different from a lake?

CONCLUSION

Drawing a conclusion is like answering the question "so what?" after reading the passage. A conclusion sums up part of the writer's message. If the passage shows that whales are dying off, you could conclude that people who live by eating and hunting whales will probably have to adjust in some way.

CHOOSE THE
BEST ANSWER

Each question is followed by five answer choices. You are asked to choose the one that is the BEST answer to the question. Remember to read all five choices before you choose your answer.

CHECK YOUR
ANSWERS

When you are ready to check your answers, use the **Answers and Explanations** at the end of each unit. Each answer is explained so that you will know why it is the BEST answer.

START A
NOTEBOOK OF
MAIN IDEAS

It's a good idea to get a notebook and write down every main idea you work with in this book. Explain the idea in your own words. Use some of the details from the passage. You also might want to jot down the Key Words and what they mean. A notebook like this is a good tool for learning anything and may help make science "belong" to you. Science ideas from TV, radio, movies, newspapers and magazines may be included. Look at the picture that shows how a page from your notebook might look.

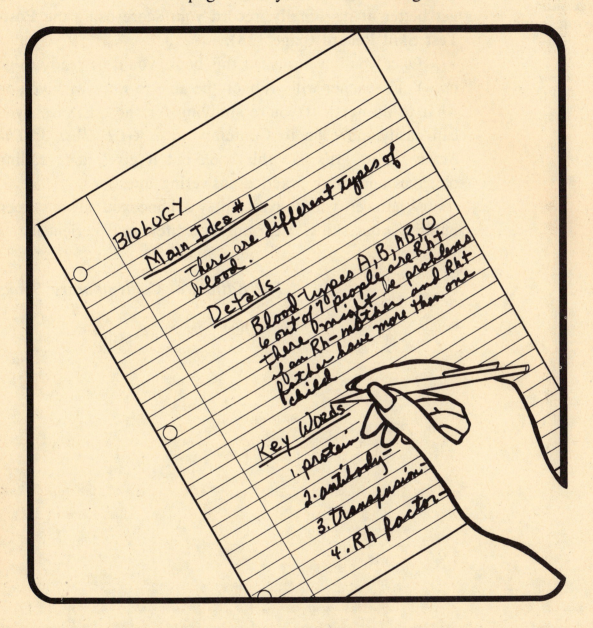

TAKE THE POST-TEST

After you have worked through all the passages and the questions, take the **Post-Test.** Like the Pre-Test, the Post-Test is made up of 25 questions from all four units of science. There are questions that follow reading passages and some that follow cartoons, graphs or charts. There are also questions that stand alone to test your science knowledge.

**CHECK YOUR
POST-TEST
ANSWERS**

**RECORD
YOUR SCORE**

YOUR NEXT STEP

You'll be able to check your answers as you did with the Pre-Test. The **Answers and Explanations** list the reading and science skills you used. If you had trouble with one kind of reading skill, go back through the book and practice. You'll get better at it. Finally, record your score using the **Post-Test Skill Record** (page 138).

Once you have finished this book, you'll be ready to go on. Your teacher will probably be able to work with you on what to do next. If you're studying for the GED test, you can easily move on to Contemporary's *GED Test 3: The Science Test*. It's like this book but it gives new reading passages and more practice answering questions.

Whatever your next step, we hope you always keep building your skills. Learning is a lifelong experience!

The Editors at Contemporary Books

PRE-TEST

The Pre-Test is for your own use. It will tell you which reading skills you already have and which reading skills you need to work on. It will also give you an idea of the kinds of science passages you will see in the book.

There are two types of questions on this test. Some questions follow a passage. The answers will come from your reading. Other questions called "discrete items" stand alone. You have to use your own experience or prior knowledge to answer a discrete item.

Place a check mark (✔) in the space next to the BEST answer. If you don't know an answer, you can guess. Take your time. There is no time limit. When you finish the Pre-Test, check your answers in the Answers and Explanations section that follows.

In the Answers and Explanations section, circle each correct answer. Then turn to page 14 to fill in the Pre-Test Skill Record.

History has shown us that man is a killer. That may be a shocking statement, but it's true. Since the 1600s, some 300 species of birds and mammals have disappeared or become extinct. The list of endangered fauna, or animal life, now has more than 650 different birds and mammals on it. Humans are to blame for the declining number of these animals.

We probably did not want this to happen. But as our way of life has changed, our actions have changed. And the animals around us have been affected. Three ways that humans harm animals are by poaching, encroachment and land abuse.

Poaching is the illegal killing or trapping of wild animals. These animals are used for meat, hides or horns, or they are sold to parks and zoos. For example, in Africa great herds of wild animals are being killed off. At one time, the white rhino of South Africa numbered less than 100. Because of strict law enforcement, and stiff penalties for game hunting, there are now 500 white rhinos.

As the human population of the world grows, people continue to encroach on, or take over, more wildlife areas. Wild animals are being pushed into parks and reserves. Their routes of migration are being blocked or changed by such things as fences, suburbs, superhighways and oil pipelines. Encroachment is almost impossible to stop and hard to control.

Another way humans endanger animal life is through land abuse. We are spoiling the land and water with chemicals and wastes. One such chemical is DDT, a pesticide that has been used by farmers for years. DDT protects crops from harmful insects and disease. But DDT stays in the soil and is carried from the fields into streams and rivers. It then poisons fish and birds. Scientists have observed a drastic decline in fish-eating birds where too much DDT is being used.

1. The passage is mainly about ways people have
   _____(1) harmed animal life with chemicals
   _____(2) blocked animal migration
   _____(3) moved into animal territory
   _____(4) captured animals illegally
   _____(5) endangered animal life

2. Fauna refers to

_____(1) flowers
_____(2) plants
_____(3) animals
_____(4) humans
_____(5) rhinos

3. As world population grows, wildlife is threatened because

_____(1) more meat is eaten
_____(2) more people visit zoos
_____(3) more land is needed
_____(4) there are more hunters
_____(5) there are more poachers

4. If people continue to encroach on wildlife, the numbers of wild animals will probably

_____(1) increase
_____(2) decrease
_____(3) remain the same
_____(4) change
_____(5) be counted

5. With strict law enforcement, governments should be able to

_____(1) stop overpopulation
_____(2) control poaching
_____(3) prevent use of chemicals
_____(4) build more parks
_____(5) stop hunting

PLANT CELL

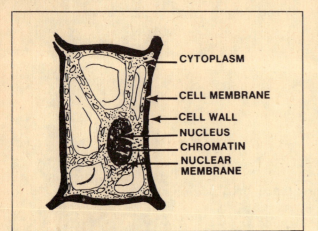

ANIMAL CELL

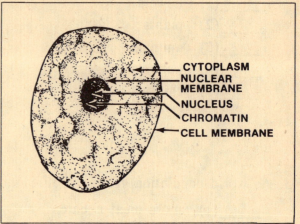

An organism is any living plant or animal. All organisms are made of living matter called protoplasm. Protoplasm varies from animal to animal and from plant to plant. It also varies within any given organism. For example, the protoplasm of human skin is different from that of the stomach lining.

Cells are the living building blocks of protoplasm. Cells can grow and reproduce. The typical animal or plant cell has three main parts. These are the nucleus, the cytoplasm and the cell membrane.

The nucleus is round. It is usually found near the center of the cell. It is also the center of the action. The nucleus controls the life of the cell. It is made up of several important materials. The most important is chromatin, which forms the chromosomes and carries the genes.

Between the nucleus and the outer edge is the cytoplasm. The cytoplasm contains proteins and fats. Molecules of food are received and processed here, or they are stored for later use.

The outer edge of the cell is called the cell membrane. It is firm and tough, but food and those things important to life can pass through it.

While animal and plant cells have similar parts, there are a few differences. Plant cells have a cell wall in addition to a cell membrane. Plant cells also have chloroplasts. Chloroplasts contain chlorophyll, the green coloring in plants. Chlorophyll helps make food for the plant through the process known as photosynthesis.

6. The passage is mainly about

_____(1) organisms

_____(2) photosynthesis

_____(3) protoplasm

_____(4) cell structure

_____(5) chromosomes

7. The living matter of all organisms is

_____(1) protoplasm

_____(2) the nucleus

_____(3) DNA

_____(4) chloroplasts

_____(5) chlorophyll

8. A plant cell is different from an animal cell because it contains

_____(1) cell membrane and chloroplast

_____(2) DNA and chromatin

_____(3) cell wall and chloroplast

_____(4) cytoplasm and a nucleus

_____(5) a nucleus and cytoplasm

9. An animal cell is unable to carry on photosynthesis because it doesn't contain

_____(1) chlorophyll

_____(2) DNA

_____(3) cytoplasm

_____(4) protoplasm

_____(5) organisms

10. You can conclude that every cell must have a nucleus

_____(1) so photosynthesis can take place
_____(2) to control the activities of the cell
_____(3) to allow food to pass through
_____(4) to store proteins and fats
_____(5) to store chloroplasts

_____

11. From the cartoon, you can conclude that pollution

_____(1) has always been a problem
_____(2) is becoming more of a problem
_____(3) makes people remember the past
_____(4) cannot be seen in the dark
_____(5) does not cause problems

_____

12. How many major blood groups are there?

_____(1) 2

_____(2) 4

_____(3) 6

_____(4) 5

_____(5) 8

_____

13. If the following objects were dropped from the same height at the same time, which would land first?

_____(1) a bowling ball

_____(2) a golf ball

_____(3) a tennis ball

_____(4) a softball

_____(5) they would all land at the same time

_____

14. A substance that can be easily found as a solid, liquid or a gas is

_____(1) iron

_____(2) mercury

_____(3) air

_____(4) water

_____(5) ozone

_____

15. Scientists who study fossils are known as

_____(1) geographers

_____(2) anthropologists

_____(3) chemists

_____(4) engineers

_____(5) paleontologists

_____

16. The electricity we use every day is

_____(1)   current electricity

_____(2)   static electricity

_____(3)   magnet electricity

_____(4)   steam electricity

_____(5)   photo electricity

_____

17. Thermal energy is

_____(1)   caused by the sun

_____(2)   used to run windmills

_____(3)   caused by high and low tides

_____(4)   stored inside the earth's crust

_____(5)   a cause of pollution

_____

18. The earth completes one rotation on its axis every

_____(1)   28 days

_____(2)   365½ days

_____(3)   9.2 years

_____(4)   12 hours

_____(5)   24 hours

A heart attack isn't always easy to recognize. Warning signs may not even be noticed by the victim. These signs can be so mild that a person thinks they are caused by other things.

There are many symptoms that warn a person of a possible heart attack. One of the main signs is constant pain in the center of the chest. This pain may spread to the shoulders, arms, neck and even the jaw. Some heart attack victims also experience nausea, sweating and extreme shortness of breath. Other victims turn pale or their lips and skin turn blue.

A person having any of these problems for longer than two minutes needs medical help right away. If the heart attack victim responds quickly to the warning signs, that person has a good chance of survival.

19. The best title for this passage is

_____(1)   Chance of Survival
_____(2)   Heart Attack Rescue
_____(3)   Turning Blue
_____(4)   Saving a Life
_____(5)   Heart Attack Symptoms

20. According to the passage, the following is NOT a major sign of a heart attack.

_____(1)   fever
_____(2)   chest pain
_____(3)   aching jaw
_____(4)   nausea
_____(5)   sweating

21. Many heart attack victims die because

_____(1)   all heart attacks are fatal
_____(2)   they don't respond to warning signs
_____(3)   they aren't healthy
_____(4)   they don't fight
_____(5)   they choose the wrong kind of doctor

22. If you have a sharp pain in your chest, you

_____(1) are having a heart attack

_____(2) are not having a heart attack

_____(3) could be having a heart attack

_____(4) have had a heart attack

_____(5) can't possibly be having a heart attack

23. The author of the passage concludes that survival for the heart attack victim depends on

_____(1) a good hospital

_____(2) an experienced nurse

_____(3) an ambulance

_____(4) a quick response

_____(5) remaining conscious

_____

24. Animals that are warm-blooded, have hair and nurse their young are

_____(1) birds

_____(2) reptiles

_____(3) fish

_____(4) mammals

_____(5) lizards

_____

Punch

"That makes it 23 known surviving examples."

25. The topic of the cartoon is

_____(1) an African safari

_____(2) endangered species

_____(3) illegal poaching

_____(4) an animal census

_____(5) careless driving

ANSWERS AND EXPLANATIONS—PRE-TEST

Main Idea	1.	**(5)** is the best answer. (1), (2), (3) and (4) are part of the main idea. They are some of the ways that man has endangered or hurt animal life.
Detail	2.	**(3)** is the best answer. Fauna refers to animal life.
Cause-Effect	3.	**(3)** is the best answer. The author writes about wildlife areas being taken over as the population grows.
Cause-Effect	4.	**(2)** is the correct answer. In paragraph two the author explains that as man moves into wildlife areas, the number of animals decreases due to such things as lack of feeding grounds and interference with migration paths.
Conclusion	5.	**(2)** is the best answer. The author suggests that poaching can be controlled through law enforcement. The example of the white rhino is given in the passage.
Main Idea	6.	**(4)** is the best answer. The structure of plant and animal cells is described throughout the selection.
Detail	7.	**(1)** is the correct answer. Protoplasm is the living matter of all organisms.
Compare-Contrast	8.	**(3)** is the correct answer. While plant and animal cells are similar, the plant cell alone has a cell wall and chloroplast.
Cause-Effect	9.	**(1)** is the best answer. Only plant cells contain chlorophyll which is necessary for the food making process known as photosynthesis.
Conclusion	10.	**(2)** is the best answer. The nucleus controls the activities of the cell.
Conclusion	11.	**(2)** is the best answer. The cartoon is showing that because there is so much pollution today, misty eyes are common.
Prior Knowledge	12.	**(2)** is the correct answer. O, A, B and AB are the four major blood groups.
Prior Knowledge	13.	**(5)** is the correct answer. The gravitational pull of the earth puts the same amount of pressure on any object regardless of its weight.

Prior Knowledge   14.   (**4**) is the best answer. Water can easily be found as ice (solid), water (liquid) or steam (gas).

Prior Knowledge   15.   (**5**) is the correct answer. An paleontologist is a scientist who studies fossils.

Prior Knowledge   16.   (**1**) is the correct answer because current electricity is used in the home as a main source of energy.

Prior Knowledge   17.   (**4**) is the correct answer. Thermal energy comes from the heat of the earth. It is caused by hot gases and molten rock within the core of the earth.

Prior Knowledge   18.   (**5**) is the correct answer. The earth completes one rotation on its axis every 24 hours.

Main Idea   19.   (**5**) is the best answer. Heart attack symptoms, such as chest pain and shortness of breath, are discussed throughout the passage.

Detail   20.   (**1**) is the correct answer. Fever is not mentioned in this passage about heart attack symptoms.

Cause-Effect   21.   (**2**) is the best answer. The author explains that many people either do not recognize heart attack warning signs or they relate them to something else such as indigestion.

Cause-Effect   22.   (**3**) is the best answer. One of the major symptoms of heart attack is pain in the center of the chest.

Conclusion   23.   (**4**) is the best answer. The reader can conclude that a quick response to any of the heart attack warning signs may save a life.

Prior Knowledge   24.   (**4**) is the correct answer. (1) birds and (3) fish have no hair. (2) reptiles and (5) lizards are cold blooded. Therefore, mammals is the correct answer.

Inference   25.   (**2**) is the best answer. The clue to the answer is in the phrase "23 known surviving examples." If only 23 examples of the species are left, the species must be endangered.

PRE-TEST ANSWER KEY

1. (5)	6. (4)	11. (2)	16. (1)	21. (2)
2. (3)	7. (1)	12. (2)	17. (4)	22. (3)
3. (3)	8. (3)	13. (5)	18. (5)	23. (4)
4. (2)	9. (1)	14. (4)	19. (5)	24. (4)
5. (2)	10. (2)	15. (5)	20. (1)	25. (2)

PRE-TEST SKILL RECORD

Directions: Fill in the Pre-Test Skill Record after you have taken the Pre-Test and have checked your answers. The Skill Record will show your strengths in science reading skills and prior knowledge.

PRE-TEST DATE: _____

Pre-Test skills	Test Questions	Total Questions	Number Correct
• Finding the Main Idea	1,6,19	3	
• Recalling Details	2,7,20	3	
• Seeing Relationships			
Cause-Effect	3,4,9, 21,22	5	
Compare-Contrast	8	1	
• Making Inferences	25	1	
• Drawing Conclusions	5,10,11,23	4	
• Using Prior Knowledge	12,13,14,15 16,17,18,24	8	
TOTAL		25	

TEST SCORE

UNIT I: BIOLOGY

Biology is the study of plants and animals—how they grow, adapt, reproduce and interact.

Directions: Read each passage. As you read, think about the ideas, facts and examples given. Study any pictures or charts that go with the passages. The Key Words will give you an idea of what the passage is about. They are used in the passage along with other new words. Look up any word that is new in the Glossary at the end of the book. You will be able to figure out many new words as you read them in the passage.

After each passage, there are five questions for you to answer. Each question builds a reading skill. Choose the BEST answer and place a check mark (✔) in the space next to it.

The Answers and Explanations begin on page 48.

BIOLOGY PASSAGE 1

KEY WORDS

spawn—(verb) to lay eggs
cycle—(noun) a series of events that repeats itself in the same order

---

Before 1798 Atlantic salmon swam up the Connecticut River to spawn. They laid their eggs in the place where they were born. Their upstream swimming stopped in 1798 because a dam was built at Turners Falls, Massachusetts (see map). The dam blocked the river. This kept the fish from returning to their place of birth. Cut off in this way from their spawning place, the salmon began to disappear from the river.

Many years passed before anyone thought seriously about bringing these fish back to the river. In the 1960s, the states along the river worked with some federal agencies to bring back the salmon. A fish ladder was built at Turners Falls. This ladder helped the fish to get around the dam and swim upstream.

FIGURE 1: A FISH LADDER

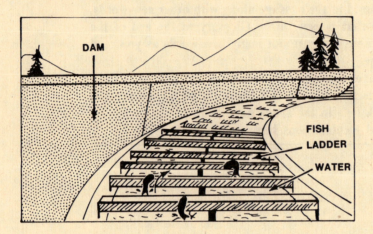

A fish ladder is a water path made in a series of small steps. The fish can jump from one step to the next until they are at the height of the water behind the dam.

The project to bring back the salmon was not an easy one. At times it even seemed hopeless. It was not until 1974 that there was any proof of success. A dead salmon was found along the shore of the river. This was the first salmon of any kind seen in the Connecticut River since 1900.

In 1975 a live Atlantic salmon was caught. In 1976 two salmon swam as far as the fish lift at the Holyoke, Massachusetts, dam (see map). A fish lift is like a fish ladder. One salmon died, but the other one was rescued by workers at a fishery. They used it for breeding with female salmon from another river. When the baby salmon hatched, they were put out into the Connecticut River.

Figure 2: PATH OF THE ATLANTIC SALMON

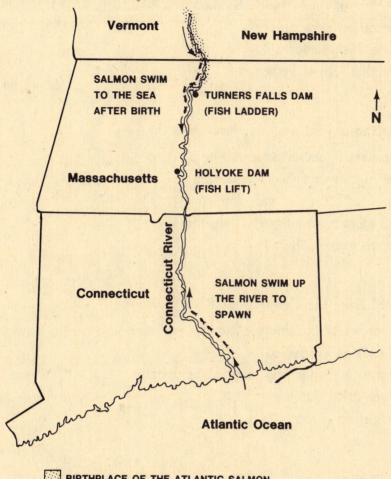

BIRTHPLACE OF THE ATLANTIC SALMON

Today, scientists have successfully bred an Atlantic salmon which can complete its life cycle in the Connecticut River. After birth, this salmon swims down the river and lives at sea for two years. By swimming up the fish lift and fish ladder, it can return to its birthplace to spawn and start another cycle of life.

Returning Atlantic salmon to the Connecticut River is a small but important victory. It shows that even when a natural resource has been lost, it can sometimes be restored. This work costs money, but the money is well spent if it preserves or even restores the original balance of nature.

1. The best title for this passage is

    _____(1)   The Return of the Atlantic Salmon
    _____(2)   Life Cycle of the Atlantic Salmon
    _____(3)   Conservation Programs
    _____(4)   Building Fish Ladders
    _____(5)   Connecticut River Fisheries

2. The first sign that the project might succeed was that

    _____(1)   government agencies began to help
    _____(2)   people no longer fished for salmon
    _____(3)   pollution of the river was stopped
    _____(4)   a dead salmon was found along the shore
    _____(5)   canneries were built

3. Salmon disappeared from the Connecticut River because

    _____(1)   the river water became too heavily polluted
    _____(2)   the river was overfished
    _____(3)   upstream migration was stopped by a dam
    _____(4)   the river dried out
    _____(5)   a drought occurred

4. Atlantic salmon spawn

    _____(1)   in the place where they were born
    _____(2)   wherever they happen to be during spawning season
    _____(3)   only at sea
    _____(4)   during their migration to the sea
    _____(5)   only in the Connecticut River

5. According to the passage you can conclude that the cost of
    conservation projects

    _____(1)   should be paid by industry
    _____(2)   must be weighed against the economic benefits
    _____(3)   can be paid with fishing license fees
    _____(4)   isn't very high
    _____(5)   is necessary to protect nature's balance

Answers start on page 48.

BIOLOGY PASSAGE 2

> **KEY WORDS**
> **cell**—(noun) the building block of living things
> **tissue**—(noun) a group of cells that look alike and do the same job
> **organ**—(noun) a group of tissues that work together
> **system**—(noun) a group of organs that work together

All living things are made up of tiny <u>cells</u>. Cells are so small that you need a microscope to see one. Yet all the basic activities of life happen within cells.

The simplest animals are just one cell. That one cell must take on all the life activities itself. Large, complex animals, including people, are made up of trillions of cells. Among so large a number, cells are able to specialize. A group of cells that look alike and do the same job is called a <u>tissue</u>. Muscle, fat and nerves are examples of tissues. Each is made up of a different kind of cell.

Various tissues may work together to do one basic job. A group of tissues working together is an <u>organ</u>. The heart is a good example of an organ. Its job is to pump the blood through the blood vessels. Muscle tissue makes up the walls of the heart and provides the movement. A slick lining tissue covers the inside of the heart. This allows blood to move through quickly. A bundle of nerve tissue in one part of the wall sets the pace for heart action. Another tissue forms a tough protective sac, or bag, around the heart. Fluid within this sac allows the heart to move easily and prevents it from rubbing against other organs of the chest. Together all of these tissues pump the blood.

THE CIRCULATORY SYSTEM

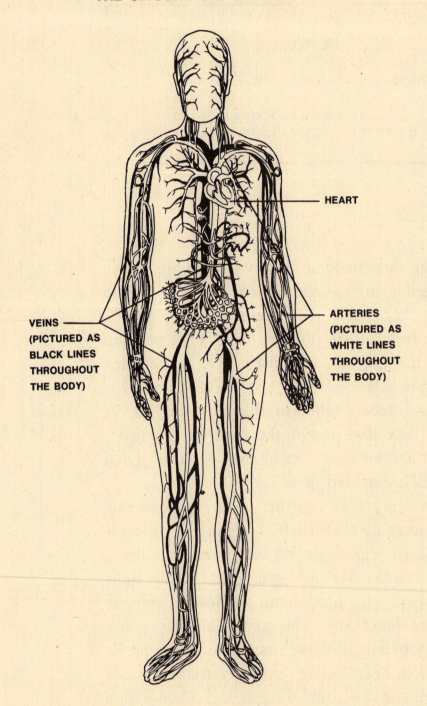

HEART

VEINS
(PICTURED AS
BLACK LINES
THROUGHOUT
THE BODY)

ARTERIES
(PICTURED AS
WHITE LINES
THROUGHOUT
THE BODY)

For still broader jobs, organs work together in systems. Humans have ten body systems. The circulatory system is one example. It is made up of the heart, arteries, veins and capillaries.

The following table shows the job and parts of the ten body systems:

HUMAN BODY SYSTEMS		
System	**Job**	**Organs**
Circulatory	Moves materials throughout the body	Heart, Arteries, Veins and Capillaries
Skeletal	Supports and protects the body	Bones and Cartilage
Muscular	Allows movement	Muscles
Digestive	Breaks down and absorbs food	Mouth, Esophagus, Stomach, Intestines, Liver and Pancreas
Excretory	Removes waste	Kidneys and Bladder
Integumentary	Gives the body a waterproof protective covering	Skin, Hair and Nails
Respiratory	Takes in oxygen and gets rid of carbon dioxide	Nasal Passages, Trachea and Lungs
Nervous	Gives control and sensation to the body	Brains, Nerves, Eyes and Ears
Endocrine	Provides internal chemical control	Hormone Producing Glands
Reproductive	Allows humans to produce children	Testes, Ovaries, Penis, Vagina and Uterus

A complex living thing, or organism, is something like a large nation. The body systems are like major industries, each one dependent on the others. The organs are like factories, with tissues being like the different production departments. Each cell, like each citizen of a well-ordered nation, does a tiny but necessary part of the work of the whole. And each in turn depends upon all the actions of the whole to provide what it needs to live.

6. This passage is mainly about

_____(1) how the heart works

_____(2) how cells work

_____(3) one-celled animals

_____(4) how the body is organized

_____(5) the ten body systems

7. A group of similar cells with the same job is called a(n)

_____(1) cell

_____(2) tissue

_____(3) organ

_____(4) system

_____(5) organism

8. The heart is an organ because

_____(1) it is made up of several different tissues with one main job

_____(2) it is made up of many cells

_____(3) it is found in the chest

_____(4) it pumps the blood throughout the body

_____(5) the rest of the body depends on it

9. The body system which cleans wastes from the body is

_____(1)   the skeletal system
_____(2)   the endocrine system
_____(3)   the digestive system
_____(4)   the reproductive system
_____(5)   the excretory system

10. After reading this passage, you can conclude that your body works so well because

_____(1)   each part has its own work and all parts depend on each other
_____(2)   each part works separately from all of the others
_____(3)   a cell has no special function
_____(4)   a tissue is made of cells which do not look alike
_____(5)   an organ is made of only one tissue

Answers start on page 48.

BIOLOGY PASSAGE 3

> ### KEY WORDS
> **extinct**—(adjective) no longer living on Earth
> **fossil**—(noun) the remains of an ancient plant or animal
> **paleontologist**—(noun) a scientist who studies fossils

For years writers have been able to thrill millions of people with stories of ancient beasts or dinosaurs. These giants ruled our planet for 140 million years. Then about 65 million years ago they disappeared. Even today, scientists are looking for reasons for this great disappearance of dinosaurs.

Interest in the mystery of these extinct, or no-longer living, animals began in 1822. During that year an English doctor and his wife found some large fossils. Later, others found jawbones of large animals as well as other fossils. By 1842, the animals became known as dinosaurs, the "terrible lizards." By the late 1800s scientists called <u>paleontologists</u> began serious studies of fossils.

SIZE AND DIET OF THREE DINOSAURS

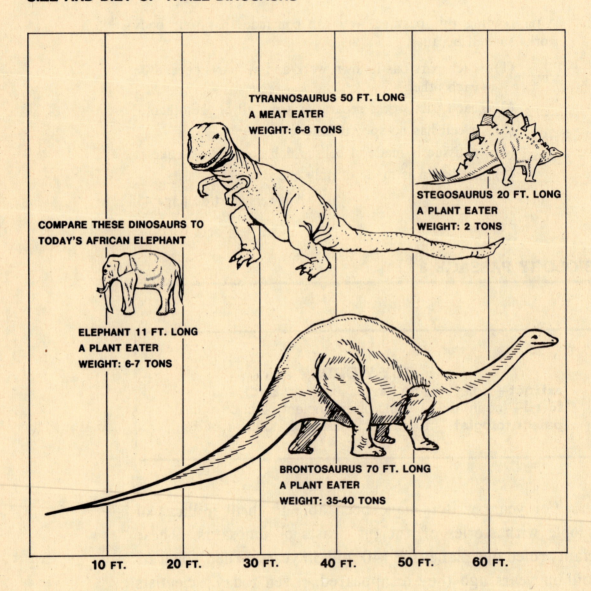

TYRANNOSAURUS 50 FT. LONG
A MEAT EATER
WEIGHT: 6-8 TONS

STEGOSAURUS 20 FT. LONG
A PLANT EATER
WEIGHT: 2 TONS

COMPARE THESE DINOSAURS TO TODAY'S AFRICAN ELEPHANT

ELEPHANT 11 FT. LONG
A PLANT EATER
WEIGHT: 6-7 TONS

BRONTOSAURUS 70 FT. LONG
A PLANT EATER
WEIGHT: 35-40 TONS

10 FT.   20 FT.   30 FT.   40 FT.   50 FT.   60 FT.

Dinosaurs were found all over the earth. Their sizes ranged from small creatures to huge 70-ton giants. Some were meat-eaters. Others ate only plants. Some moved about on four feet, others on two. Recently, scientists discovered an ancient reptile with an arm and hand over eight feet long. The hand alone measured more than 24 inches. The design of the hand bones indicates that this meat-eater would tear its victim apart before eating it.

For millions of years, most animals on Earth were dinosaurs. What happened to these animals? What took place on this planet during the time of these great beasts? Why did they all die off? Man, of course, was not yet present to record what occurred.

Today scientists offer some explanations. One theory is that dinosaurs died because of drastic changes in climate. Cold-blooded as well as warm-blooded dinosaurs with no fur or feathers suffered from extreme cold. Eventually the weather killed them off. Another idea is that increasing numbers of smaller animals such as rodents ate the dinosaur eggs. Gradually, they eliminated the large beasts.

Could this happen again? Could we experience a disaster such as this in our lifetimes? Paleontologists are still searching for an explanation for the sudden death of the dinosaurs. We don't have an answer yet.

11.   The best title for this passage is
_____(1)   65 Million Years Ago on Earth
_____(2)   Ruled by the Animal Kingdom
_____(3)   What Happened to Ancient Animals?
_____(4)   Paleontologists on the Scene
_____(5)   A New Theory

12. The remains of ancient animals or plants are known as

_____(1)   dinosaurs
_____(2)   reptiles
_____(3)   giants
_____(4)   fossils
_____(5)   lizards

13. Scientists are not sure how dinosaurs lived or why they became extinct because

_____(1)   there are no dinosaur fossils
_____(2)   the animals are too large to study
_____(3)   dinosaurs died off before humans lived
_____(4)   equipment used to study dinosaurs is not very good
_____(5)   scientists can never be sure of anything

14. Dinosaurs could be described as

_____(1)   small creatures
_____(2)   70-ton giants
_____(3)   meat-eaters
_____(4)   plant-eaters
_____(5)   all of the above

15. From this passage you can conclude that

_____(1)   scientists know why dinosaurs disappeared
_____(2)   scientists do not know why dinosaurs disappeared
_____(3)   dinosaurs disappeared because of drastic changes in climate
_____(4)   dinosaurs disappeared because rodents ate their eggs
_____(5)   dinosaurs never really disappeared

Answers start on page 48.

BIOLOGY PASSAGE 4

KEY WORDS

stimulant—(noun) a drug that speeds up (stimulates) body functions

depressant—(noun) a drug that slows down (depresses) body functions

hallucinogen—(noun) a drug that makes the user see or feel things that aren't really there

Many people take drugs every day but don't know it. For instance, people who drink coffee are taking a drug. The drug in coffee is called caffeine. Caffeine is a stimulant. A stimulant is a drug that speeds up (stimulates) body functions. That is why most people feel more awake after they drink coffee.

Another common stimulant is the nicotine in tobacco. Though many people believe smoking calms their nerves, it actually makes them more nervous.

In many cases, the combined effect of taking two drugs at once is greater than we would expect. It is often more than just the sum of the separate effects of each drug.

Try taking the pulse of a friend or co-worker who smokes before a coffee break. After the person smokes a cigarette and drinks a cup of coffee, take his or her pulse again. You'll probably note a big increase in the heart rate.

A drug which has the opposite effect of a stimulant is called a depressant. A depressant is a drug that slows down (depresses) body functions. Alcohol is a depressant. That is why people who drink too much alcohol speak and move more slowly than they normally do. It is also why many people fall asleep after drinking too much alcohol.

Tranquilizers and sleeping pills are other depressants. Combining alcohol and sleeping pills is extremely dangerous. Again, the effects of each are multiplied causing body func-

SOME COMMON DRUGS

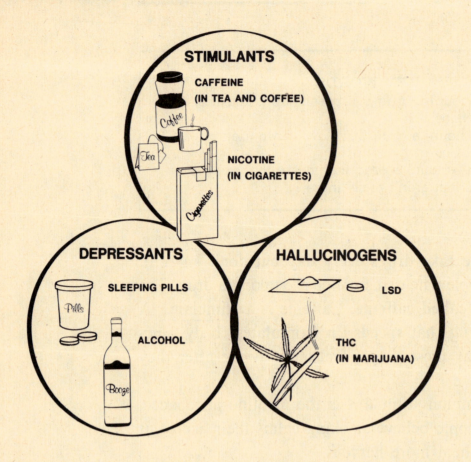

tions to slow down until they stop. Many people, including actress Marilyn Monroe, have died of this combination.

A third group of drugs is the hallucinogens. These drugs cause people to hallucinate, that is, see or feel things that aren't really there. LSD is the most famous and powerful hallucinogen but THC, the active chemical in marijuana and hashish, is also hallucinogenic. Usually, smoking marijuana only makes the user feel a little strange, not too different from the effects of drinking alcohol. Some people, though, experience anxiety, unreasonable fear and even panic.

Problems can arise from using even these common drugs. One is dependence, whether it is the person who can't get started in the morning without a cup of coffee or the one who can't relax without a drink.

Another problem is side effects. It is now known that smoking is directly related to lung cancer and other respiratory diseases. Alcohol harms the liver and brain. Finally, there is the problem of multiplying a drug effect by combining drugs, as with alcohol and sleeping pills.

16. The main idea of this passage is

_____(1) coffee causes brain damage

_____(2) we always know when we are taking drugs

_____(3) drugs should only be taken with a doctor's permission

_____(4) alcohol is used to make you sleep

_____(5) our everyday diet often contains drugs

17. A drug that slows body systems down is

_____(1) a stimulant

_____(2) caffeine

_____(3) a depressant

_____(4) speed

_____(5) LSD

18. One of the most commonly used drugs that is a stimulant is

_____(1) alcohol

_____(2) sleeping pills

_____(3) caffeine

_____(4) marijuana

_____(5) aspirin

19. Taking two drugs from the same drug group (such as stimulants or depressants) at the same time

_____(1) can multiply their effect dangerously

_____(2) allows one drug to offset the effect of the other

_____(3) keeps the user from getting sick

_____(4) doubles your fun

_____(5) doesn't increase or decrease the effect of the drugs

20. After reading this passage, you can conclude that

_____(1)   most cancer is caused by drugs
_____(2)   marijuana is the same as alcohol
_____(3)   most people use drugs in some form
_____(4)   most people avoid using drugs
_____(5)   people dislike drugs

Answers start on page 49.

BIOLOGY PASSAGE 5

KEY WORDS
trait—(noun) a physical characteristic
heredity—(noun) the "passing on" of family traits
genetics—(noun) the study of how heredity works
chromosome—(noun) a rod-shaped body in an animal or
 plant cell nucleus that holds the hereditary information
gene—(noun) a unit of information in the chromosomes
 about a particular trait, such as eye color, hair
 color or height

"Congratulations," said the doctor. "Mary is doing fine. The baby looks like her mother but has her daddy's eyes."

Words like these are said many times each day around the world. Our physical <u>traits</u> (such as hair color, blood type and height) are based on the traits of our mothers and fathers and their families before them. The "passing on" of family traits is known as <u>heredity</u>. The study of how heredity works is called <u>genetics</u>.

All living things are made of cells. With a microscope, we can look at a cell and its parts. In the core or nucleus of each cell are rod-shaped bodies called <u>chromosomes</u>. Every organism within a species has the same number of chromosomes. For example, all corn plants have 20 chromosomes. A certain species of worm has only two chromosomes. Some crabs have up to 200. Humans have 46 chromosomes in each cell of their bodies.

Each person begins as one cell, the union of an egg cell from the mother and a sperm cell from the father. The sperm and egg each contribute 23 chromosomes to make up the original 46. As this first cell develops into a person these 46 chromosomes are duplicated over and over again in every cell of the body.

Chromosomes contain the hereditary information which determines how the body will look and how it will work. This information is chemically coded into a molecule called DNA. Each bit of information about a particular trait is called a gene. The chromosomes may be thought of as strings of genes, with each chromosome containing information about many traits.

The 46 chromosomes in a human cell come in 23 pairs. One member of each pair comes from each parent. Both

A PAIR OF CHROMOSOMES

Other chromosome pairs will be longer or shorter and will have different markings.

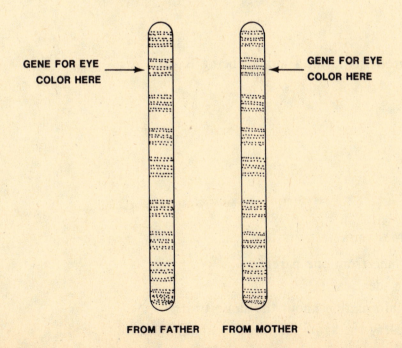

GENE FOR EYE COLOR HERE →

← GENE FOR EYE COLOR HERE

FROM FATHER   FROM MOTHER

members of a pair carry information about the same traits but the information may be different. For example, each chromosome of a pair carries a gene for eye color. But one of them may carry a gene for blue eyes and one may carry a gene for brown eyes.

Obviously, if both genes for a trait are the same, there is no question as to the result. Two genes for blue eyes produce a blue-eyed individual. Two genes for brown eyes produce brown eyes. But what happens when the genes are different? A person with one gene for brown eyes and one gene for blue eyes will have brown eyes. The gene for brown eyes is said to be dominant. The gene for blue eyes is recessive. It is there but it is not shown. It may show up in the next generation, however, in combination with another gene for blue eyes. Two brown-eyed parents can have a blue-eyed baby if each parent carries a hidden gene for blue eyes.

21. The passage is mainly about
_____(1)   children
_____(2)   genes
_____(3)   DNA
_____(4)   chromosomes
_____(5)   genetics

22. The number of chromosomes in a human being is
_____(1)   20
_____(2)   23
_____(3)   46
_____(4)   64
_____(5)   200

23. Human chromosomes come in pairs that
_____(1)   both come from one parent
_____(2)   contain identical DNA
_____(3)   carry information about the same traits
_____(4)   must carry the same information about each trait
_____(5)   aren't important because all chromosomes look alike

24. What combination of parents could have a blue-eyed baby?

_____(1)   two blue-eyed parents

_____(2)   two brown-eyed parents

_____(3)   one brown eyed parent and one blue-eyed parent

_____(4)   all of the above

_____(5)   none of the above

25. In hair color, brown is dominant and blonde is recessive. From the information in the passage, you can conclude that a blonde couple

_____(1)   can't have blonde children

_____(2)   can't have brown-haired children

_____(3)   can't have any children

_____(4)   could have both brown-haired and blonde children

_____(5)   will usually but not always have blonde children

Answers start on page 49.

BIOLOGY PASSAGE 6

KEY WORDS

suffocation—(noun) death caused by a lack of air
symptom—(noun) a sign of some problem or illness

Each year more than 2,000 people in the United States die from <u>suffocation</u>. Suffocation is caused by the blocking of the air passage. A person who can't get air will die in a matter of minutes unless immediate action is taken.

Choking is caused by something, often food, which is caught in the throat. It creates a blockage in the trachea, or windpipe. Because of the blockage, oxygen can't enter or leave the lungs. The victim can't breathe and also may not be able to speak. She or he will die of suffocation in about four minutes unless someone uses the Heimlich maneuver to save the person's life.

Obvious <u>symptoms</u> of choking are great difficulty in

speaking or breathing. The person loses his normal healthy coloring. Skin tones may turn from gray to blue. The victim may signal when he can't speak. He will grab his neck to show that he is choking (Figure 1). If help is not given, the person will collapse.

Figure 1. A sign of choking.

This drawing and those on the following pages have been reprinted with the permission of the Massachusetts Department of Mental Health.

If others are present, someone should go for help. In the meantime, immediate attempts to restore breathing should begin. Look in the victim's mouth for food or anything that is blocking the throat.

The Heimlich maneuver can be used whether the victim is standing, sitting or lying down. If the choking person is standing, the rescuer stands behind and wraps his arms

Figure 2. The standing rescue position.

around the victim (Figure 2). The rescuer makes a fist and places the thumb side against the victim's abdomen slightly above the area of the navel and below the rib cage. With the other hand he grasps the fist, and with a quick upward thrust, presses into the abdomen of the victim (Figure 3). It is often necessary to repeat these motions several times.

Figure 3. Press into the abdomen while victim is standing.

If the victim is seated, the rescuer stands behind the chair and uses the same procedures as though both were standing.

If the person who is choking is lying down, the procedure is slightly different. The victim should be lying on his back.

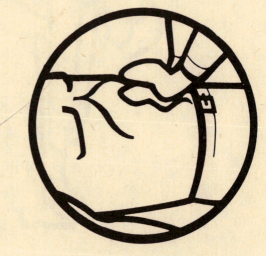

Figure 5. Press into the abdomen while the victim is lying down.

Figure 4. The lying rescue position.

The rescuer faces the victim and kneels, as shown in Figure 4. Care must be taken not to rest on the victim's hips. The legs of the patient should be between the legs of the rescuer. The hands of the rescuer are placed on top of each other and rest on the abdomen of the victim. The heel of the bottom hand should be slightly above the navel and below the rib cage. Using the heel of the hand, quick upward thrusts are pressed into the victim's abdomen (Figure 5). It may be necessary to repeat this several times. Be sure to look into the victim's mouth often. The food or blocking object should be removed as soon as it can be seen.

The Heimlich maneuver is easy to learn and, if used correctly, could save a life.

26. The best title for this passage is

_____(1) How to Prevent Suffocation
_____(2) Heimlich to the Rescue
_____(3) Avoid Suffocation by Proper Breathing
_____(4) The Heimlich Maneuver: A Life Saving Move
_____(5) Suffocation in the United States

27. A person can live without air entering the lungs for approximately

_____(1) three minutes
_____(2) two minutes
_____(3) three seconds
_____(4) four minutes
_____(5) fifteen minutes

28. If a person is having difficulty breathing, we

_____(1) know they are choking
_____(2) can tell it is a heart attack
_____(3) can assume it is a seizure
_____(4) know it's allergies
_____(5) cannot always tell what the problem is

29. If a choking person is being helped, someone else

_____(1) should make others look away
_____(2) should check to see what was eaten
_____(3) should go for professional help
_____(4) should get their hat and coat
_____(5) should notify the next of kin

30.   From reading this passage, you can conclude that

_____(1)   the Heimlich maneuver is useless

_____(2)   the Heimlich maneuver is done the same way on all victims

_____(3)   the Heimlich maneuver can save many victims of suffocation

_____(4)   the Heimlich maneuver can only be performed by a doctor

_____(5)   the Heimlich maneuver is very difficult to learn

Answers start on page 50.

BIOLOGY PASSAGE 7

KEY WORDS

kingdom—(noun) one of the two major groups of living things

phylum—(plural, phyla; noun) a group of related plant or animal classes

genus—(noun) division of a family of plants or animals

species—(noun) the most closely related group of plants or animals

---

People have always put living things into groups. A group of birds could include ducks, pigeons, sparrows and eagles. They all have wings and can fly. We also know that butterflies can fly, but we also know they are not birds. Putting things into groups is part of human nature.

Biologists do the same thing, but their groups are more carefully made. What they do is called classification. Linnaeus, an 18th century biologist, divided all Life into two groups. He called these the plant and animal kingdoms. Then he broke the kingdoms down into groups called phyla. Each phylum was broken down into classes. The classes were broken down into orders and the orders into families.

He broke each family into genera (singular, genus.) These were then broken down into species, the most closely related groups.

Animals or plants of the same species look alike and most often breed only with each other. When naming a species, we use both its genus name and its species name. The genus is a Latin noun and the species is usually a Latin adjective which describes the noun.

For example, the house cat is *Felis domesticus*. *Felis* is the Latin noun which means cat. *Domesticus* is the Latin adjective which means "of the house." *Felis leo* is the lion and *Felis tigris* is the tiger. These animals have similar bodies, so they are all put into one genus.

The cat family, along with the dog family, bears, seals and other meat-eating animals make up the order *Carnivora*. It is not just the fact of eating meat, but also having similar bones and teeth which places a family in this order.

All of these animals share certain traits with other animals in different orders. All the orders of animals with hair or fur which give birth to live young and have milk glands to feed them are in the class *Mammalia*.

A class is a large group, but a phylum is even larger. The mammals belong to the same phylum as the birds, fish, reptiles and amphibians. They all have a backbone, so they are part of the phylum *Vertebrata*.

Vertebrates have one of the many basic body plans of the animal kingdom. They are very different from grasshoppers or lobsters, two animals which have another body plan and belong to the phylum *Arthropoda*. Still, vertebrates and arthropods and all of the other phyla of animals are more like each other than they are like plants, the other great kingdom.

People, too, are more like grasshoppers than plants. They are more like cats than grasshoppers. This likeness is shown in the classification chart that follows:

CLASSIFICATIONS: PEOPLE, CATS AND GRASSHOPPERS			
	People	**Cats**	**Grasshoppers**
Kingdom	Animal	Animal	Animal
Phylum	Vertebrata	Vertebrata	Arthropoda
Class	Mammalia	Mammalia	Insecta
Order	Primates	Carnivora	Orthoptera
Family	Homonidae	Felidae	Acrididae
Genus	Homo	Felis	Schistocerca
Species	sapiens	domesticus	americana

31. A good title for this passage is

_____(1) *Felis Tigris*
_____(2) Grouping Living Things
_____(3) Family Groups
_____(4) Up the Ladder
_____(5) The Living Beast

32. A group of related genera make up a(n)

_____(1) phylum
_____(2) class
_____(3) family
_____(4) order
_____(5) species

33. Cats, dogs, bears and seals belong to the order *Carnivora,* because

_____(1) they all eat meat
_____(2) they have similar diets, teeth and bone structures
_____(3) they all eat meat and plants
_____(4) they all live in cold climates and eat meat
_____(5) all of the above

34. If two kinds of animal share the same kind of behavior, like flying,

_____(1) they must be in the same family
_____(2) they must be in the same order
_____(3) they must be in the same phylum
_____(4) they must be closely related
_____(5) they may not be in the same group at all

35. According to the passage, you can conclude that the more groups two animals share

_____(1) the more alike they are
_____(2) the more distantly related they are
_____(3) the more they'll fight
_____(4) the more they compete for food
_____(5) the less likely they are to eat each other

Answers start on page 50.

BIOLOGY PASSAGE 8

> **KEY WORDS**
> **photosynthesis**—(noun) the food-making process of plants
> **chlorophyll**—(noun) the green substance in plants that makes photosynthesis possible

Each day the sun sends down energy in the form of light. This energy is free. Our bodies use the sun's energy to make vitamin D. Plants use light energy to make food and to grow. The toast or cereal you had this morning was available because of sunlight. The coffee, juice or milk we drink today is ours because of the sun. The fish or meat we enjoy for lunch or dinner are products of the sun's energy.

Our sun, 93 million miles away, causes many things to happen when it bathes the earth in its rays. The sun warms the earth and provides energy so that plants can make food.

This food-making process is called photosynthesis.

For years we have been aware of the close relationship of sun and plants. Only recently, however, have we been able to understand it. Scientists have found out that the food-making process in plants is quite complex. However, we can say it easily in words. A green plant takes in carbon dioxide and water to make sugar (food) and oxygen. The energy or power for this process comes from the sun.

PHOTOSYNTHESIS

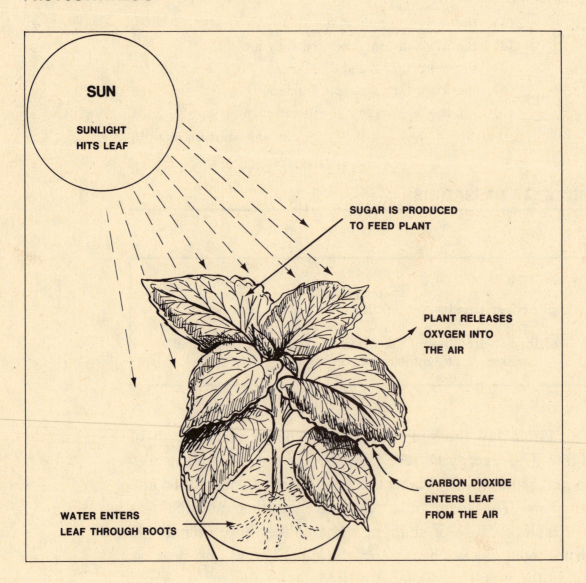

Have you ever wondered why most of our plants have green leaves? The green color comes from chlorophyll. It must be present for the food-making process to take place. Chlorophyll is useless by itself, but when present in the plant, it combines carbon dioxide and water to make food for the plant. It also makes oxygen that we breathe. We breathe in the oxygen and breathe out carbon dioxide. The plant then takes in the carbon dioxide. This is known as a cycle.

As the plant carries on the process of photosynthesis, it produces more food for itself and its growth. We enjoy that growth not only for its beauty, but also for its use as food. Farmers harvest the crops at the peak of their growth. We may eat them as they come from the field in the case of fruits and vegetables. Or they may have to be processed, as is the case with grains. We may feed them to livestock and poultry to provide the meat, milk and eggs in our menu. Regardless of the form in which we eat it, all of our food energy comes originally from the sun through photosynthesis.

36. The best title for this passage is

_____(1) Using Chlorophyll
_____(2) Vitamins from the Sun
_____(3) The World Food Shortage
_____(4) Energy from the Sun
_____(5) The Beauty of Plants

37. Sunshine causes our bodies to make

_____(1) vitamin B
_____(2) vitamin C
_____(3) vitamin D
_____(4) vitamin E
_____(5) none of the above

38. The author of this passage suggests that

_____(1)   we would not be alive except for the sun

_____(2)   the sun is necessary for life

_____(3)   man needs the sun to survive

_____(4)   all of our food directly or indirectly comes from the sun

_____(5)   all of the above

39. Oxygen, the gas we breathe, is

_____(1)   used up in photosynthesis

_____(2)   given off by plants

_____(3)   needed for photosynthesis

_____(4)   not a factor in the plant cycle

_____(5)   what makes plants grow

40. Reading the passage leads you to conclude that the process of photosynthesis is

_____(1)   important because it provides us with food

_____(2)   not needed

_____(3)   not well understood

_____(4)   highly overrated

_____(5)   not a cycle

Answers start on page 51.

BIOLOGY PASSAGE 9

KEY WORDS

protein—(noun) one of the basic chemicals found in all living things

antibody—(noun) a substance in the blood which attacks foreign proteins and which helps the body fight off infection or disease

transfusion—(noun) giving blood directly from one person to another

Rh factor—(noun) a protein found in the blood of most people (Rh+) and not found in the blood of some people (Rh−); an inherited trait

Each of us is unique, one of a kind. Not only our looks and personalities are different, but also the very proteins which make up our flesh. Our bodies recognize the <u>proteins</u> they make and will develop <u>antibodies</u> to attack any foreign protein. Antibodies are part of the system that protects us against disease germs.

Although unique, we are all enough alike that it is possible to take blood from a healthy person and give it to someone who is sick or injured. This process is called <u>transfusion</u>.

When doctors first started doing transfusions, they quickly learned that two blood proteins, which were simply called "A" and "B," complicated the process. Some people have protein A in their blood and so are called Type A. Others have protein B, so are called Type B. A few people have both proteins. They are Type AB. Many people have neither protein and are called Type O, which really should be understood as Type zero.

Remember that a person's body will attack any kind of protein which the body doesn't make, just as if it were a germ. Now look at the following table.

BLOOD TYPES			
Blood Type	Contains Protein	Can Accept Blood from Type	Can Donate Blood to Type
A	A	A or O	A or AB
B	B	B or O	B or AB
AB	A and B	all types	only AB
O	neither	only O	all types

Since Type O has neither blood protein, there is nothing to cause a reaction in anyone. Therefore, Type O individuals can safely donate blood to people of any blood type and are called Universal Donors. On the other hand, individuals with Type AB blood can safely receive blood from anyone because neither protein is foreign to them. Type AB people are called Universal Recipients.

In most cases, a person receiving the wrong type of blood in a transfusion would not have a bad reaction at that time. But after this first transfusion, the body would begin to make antibodies to fight off the foreign blood protein. Problems would begin if another transfusion of the wrong type blood were given. This second transfusion could cause the blood cells to clump together and block the blood vessels. When blood vessels to the brain or heart are blocked, it can result in brain damage or death.

Another blood protein was discovered because doctors saw bad reactions sometimes, even in transfusions that were properly matched A to A or O to O.   This protein, also found in rhesus monkeys, is the Rh factor. About six out of seven people have this protein. They are Rh positive (Rh+). The seventh person lacks the protein and is Rh negative (Rh−).

The Rh factor makes it harder to find a blood donor. For a woman who plans to have children, it can present an even more serious problem. Blood type is hereditary and Rh+ is the dominant form. This means if an Rh− woman marries an Rh+ man, their children will most likely be Rh+. Ordinarily, the blood of a developing baby in the womb doesn't mix with the mother's blood. However, accidents during pregnancy and the process of birth itself can allow the baby's blood to enter the mother's bloodstream. If she is Rh− and the baby is Rh+, she will develop antibodies to attack the foreign protein. If these antibodies get into the baby's bloodstream, they can cause the baby's blood cells to clump together and block the blood vessels.

A first child is usually safely born before its Rh− mother develops enough antibodies to harm it. Later babies, though, run greater and greater risk of brain damage and other birth defects caused by their mother's reaction to their blood.

41. The main idea of this passage is

_____(1) blood transfusions
_____(2) giving birth
_____(3) Rh factors
_____(4) blood problems
_____(5) blood types

42. According to the table a person from blood group B can receive

_____(1) group O only
_____(2) group B only
_____(3) groups B and O
_____(4) group A only
_____(5) any blood group

43. The Rh factor is particularly important

_____(1) during the first pregnancy
_____(2) during the second pregnancy
_____(3) to the universal donor
_____(4) to the universal recipient
_____(5) to people with blood Type O

44. According to the table a person from blood group A can give
     blood to a person in

_____(1) group A
_____(2) group B
_____(3) group AB
_____(4) group A or B
_____(5) group A or AB

45. From the passage the reader can conclude that

_____(1) Rh− individuals should not have children
_____(2) most newborn children need a blood transfusion
_____(3) both parents should have the same Rh factor
_____(4) it is imporatant to be aware of the different blood
            groups
_____(5) it is best to have Type O blood so you can give to all

Answers start on page 51.

ANSWERS AND EXPLANATIONS—BIOLOGY

1. (**1**) is the best answer. When you look for a title think of the main idea. What is the main idea in this passage? It is the return of the Atlantic salmon. In the passage, the life cycle (2), conservation (3), fish ladders (4), and the Connecticut River (5) are mentioned. But each of these things is a detail. Details support main ideas. The main idea is the return of the salmon to a river where it once lived.

2. (**4**) is the best answer. (3) is not true. There is no mention of pollution in the passage. (5) is not true. There is no mention of canneries in the passage. (2) is not true because people stopped fishing for salmon in the river many years ago. (1) is not true because it was not the first sign. (4) is true because it is mentioned in the passage as the first sign.

3. (**3**) is the best answer. The river was changed by the dam that was built at Turners Falls, Massachusetts, in 1798. Find this answer in the first paragraph.

4. (**1**) is the correct answer. The passage says that the Atlantic Salmon has to return to its place of birth in order to spawn. This is a detail stated at the beginning of the passage.

5. (**5**) is the best answer. While other answers may be true, only (5) can be drawn from the passage. The size of the costs (4) are not mentioned. Neither are sources of funding, (1) and (3). This leaves the choice between (2) and (5) and the passage does not limit the value of conservation to economic benefits.

6. (**4**) is the best answer. While each of the other items is mentioned in the passage, the idea which ties them all together is how parts are organized into more and more complex wholes.

7. (**2**) is the correct answer. This definition of tissue is given in the second paragraph and in the list of Key Words.

8. (**1**) is the correct answer. This definition of an organ is given in the third paragraph and in the list of Key Words.

9. (**5**) is the correct answer. This fact can be found in the table Human Body Systems.

10. (**1**) is the correct answer. In the last paragraph of the passage, your body is compared to a nation in which each part has a function, and all parts depend on each other. None of the other statements are correct.

11. (**3**) is the best answer. The passage is about ancient animals. It is

not about (4) paleontologists, (1) 65 million years ago, (2) the "rule" of the animals or (5) a new theory.

12. **(4)** is the correct answer. This detail can be found by reading the Key Words or the second paragraph. In the passage, the reader must draw the conclusion that the remains of ancient animals are known as fossils.

13. **(3)** is the best answer. The passage states that man was not yet present to record what occurred. (1) and (2) can be ruled out based on what is said in the passage. (4) is not mentioned in the passage. (5) can be ruled out because although scientists do not have *all* the answers, they have found out *some* facts about dinosaurs.

14. **(5)** is the correct answer. The passage lists each of the details given in choices (1), (2), (3) and (4) as descriptions of different kinds of dinosaurs.

15. **(2)** is the correct answer. The passage states that paleontologists are still searching for the answer. (1) is not true; (2) and (3) are listed in the passage as theories which have not been proven; (5) is not true.

16. **(5)** is the best answer. Read the first sentence in the passage. It says "Many people take drugs every day but don't know it." This is the main idea of the passage. Look for the main idea in the first sentence as you are reading. You can sometimes find it there.

17. **(3)** is the correct answer. To "slow down" is to depress. A drug that depresses is called a depressant. Look for this information in the fourth paragraph in the passage or in the Key Words list.

18. **(3)** is the correct answer. Caffeine is found in coffee and tea. Many people do not drink coffee or tea because of the caffeine. The relationship between coffee and caffeine is mentioned in the first paragraph.

19. **(1)** is the correct answer. This is stated in the second, fifth and final paragraphs.

20. **(3)** is the best answer. Each day we take drugs into our bodies if we use stimulants or depressants such as coffee or alcohol. The reader can reach this conclusion after reading the passage.

21. **(5)** is the best answer. In general, the passage is about genetics. Within the passage there is information on (4) chromosomes, (3) DNA and (2) genes and the effect they have on the characteristics of (1) children.

22. **(3)** is the correct answer. This is a detail that can be found in the fourth paragraph. Note that (2) is incorrect because 23 chromosomes come from each parent to make a total of 46.

23. (**3**) is the correct answer. This is stated in the text and pictured in the drawing. (2) and (4) amount to the same idea, that the look-alike chromosomes are identical in content. This is clearly not true from the example.

24. (**4**) is the correct answer. Blue eye color is recessive. Any brown-eyed individual may carry a hidden gene for blue eyes, which could show up in his or her children.

25. (**2**) is the correct answer. If you understand that anyone with even one dominant gene will show the dominant trait, it is plain that you must conclude neither of the blonde couple has any dominant brown genes. Therefore, they cannot pass on brown genes to their children.

26. (**4**) is the best answer. The passage is about the Heimlich maneuver, a technique to stop choking and save a life. Note that the best title has two parts. It is about the Heimlich maneuver and about saving lives. It is better than (2) or (5).

27. (**4**) is the best answer. This information is contained in the passage in the second paragraph. The amount of time a person can live without air is a detail in this passage.

28. (**5**) is the best answer. This information is implied in the passage. Although it would be easy to tell when a person is choking if there is a signal, it is not always easy to tell why a person is not breathing properly. Sometimes this is a sign of a heart attack. The person who is choking can give the Heimlich sign to let those around know what is happening.

29. (**3**) is the best answer. The choking person should receive help right away. But others should try to find a doctor to give further treatment.

30. (**3**) is the correct answer. According to the passage, (1), (2) and (5) are not true. In addition, anyone who studies it can learn to perform this life-saving action, so (4) is not true. Only choice (3) is a conclusion which may be drawn from this passage.

31. (**2**) is the best answer. The passage is about how plant and animal life is organized into orderly groups.

32. (**3**) is the correct answer. This detail can be found in the second paragraph.

33. (**2**) is the correct answer. The passage states that these animals belong to *Carnivora* not only because they all eat meat, but also because their bones and teeth are similar.

34. (**5**) is the correct answer. The passage gives the example of birds and butterflies. Both have wings and fly. Because of other differences in their body plans, though, they are not grouped together.

35. **(1)** is the correct answer. Physical similarity is the basis for classifying animals into groups.

36. **(4)** is the correct answer. (1), (2) and (5) are details found in the passage. (3) is not mentioned at all in the passage. Both the first and last paragraphs state that the energy needed to make our food comes from the sun, so (4) is the best title or main idea.

37. **(3)** is the correct answer. You can find this answer in the third sentence of the first paragraph. It is a detail concerning the value of the sun to the human body.

38. **(5)** is the best answer. The author of the passage suggests several things. The author suggests that (1) we need the sun to live, (2) the sun is necessary for life, (3) man needs the sun to survive and (4) all our food comes from the sun in some way. Therefore, all of these answers are true.

39. **(2)** is the correct answer. In the relationship between plants and oxygen, oxygen is given off by plants. This happens after the plants have taken in carbon dioxide. Oxygen is given off during photosynthesis. Find the description of this relationship in the third paragraph and in the diagram.

40. **(1)** is the best answer. The process of photosynthesis provides food for plant growth. The growth of the plant provides food for people. Photosynthesis is one of the many important life cycles.

41. **(5)** is the best answer. Although answers (1), (2), (3) and (4) are mentioned in the passage, none of them is the main idea. Instead, each of them is a detail. Each is supporting the main idea, blood types.

42. **(3)** is the best answer. You can find this answer on the table. Find the column for "Blood Type." Now look for "B" in the column. Look across the line to the third column. You will see the letters "B" and "O."

43. **(2)** is the correct answer. The Rh factor is described in the passage. It is described as a protein. If a man who has this protein in his blood marries a woman who does not, their second child may need new blood. This can be done with a blood change, or transfusion.

44. **(5)** is the correct answer. You can find this answer in the table. Look for this answer in the fourth column in the table. It is on the first line across from blood Type "A."

45. **(4)** is the best answer. This answer calls for a conclusion on the part of the reader. Answers (1), (2) and (3) are false. They do not agree with the information in the passage. Answer (5) is not implied, or suggested, in the passage. You are left with answer (4), which is a thought that the writer implies.

UNIT II: EARTH SCIENCE

Earth science is the study of our planet—its characteristics, structure, composition, movements and atmosphere.

Directions: Read each passage. As you read, think about the ideas, facts and examples given. Study any pictures or charts that go with the passages. The Key Words will give you an idea of what the passage is about. They are used in the passage along with other new words. Look up any word that is new in the Glossary at the end of the book. You will be able to figure out many new words as you read them in the passage.

After each passage, there are five questions for you to answer. Each question builds a reading skill. Make a check mark (✔) next to the BEST answer for each question.

The Answers and Explanations begin on page 81.

EARTH SCIENCE PASSAGE 1

KEY WORDS

atmosphere—(noun) the colorless, odorless gases that surround the earth

hydrosphere—(noun) all the water that is part of the earth

What do you think of when you hear the word "Earth?" Most of us think of the solid ground. We might think of soil or of the planet we live on. When scientists speak of Earth they think of three different parts. These three parts are the atmosphere, the hydrosphere and the land itself.

The atmosphere is the gases that surround our planet. It is the air we breathe. Oxygen and nitrogen are the two gases that make up most of the atmosphere. There are also small amounts of carbon dioxide, hydrogen and many other gases. The earth's atmosphere extends up about 275 miles.

The atmosphere is very important. It is the air we breathe, but it also screens out much of the sun's light. Sunlight is necessary for all life. Too much sunlight can be harmful. Without the atmosphere to protect us from the sun, the earth would be a lifeless desert.

The hydrosphere is all the water that is part of the earth. Lakes, rivers and oceans all belong to the hydrosphere. We often think of our planet as being mostly dry land. In fact, the globe has much more water covering it than land. 70% of the earth's surface is covered with water and only 30% with land.

The third part of the earth is the land itself. The surface of the earth where we live is only a thin outer layer. This outer layer is called the earth's crust. Mountains, deserts and valleys are all part of the crust. If you imagine our planet as an apple, the crust would be the skin of the apple.

LAYERS OF THE EARTH

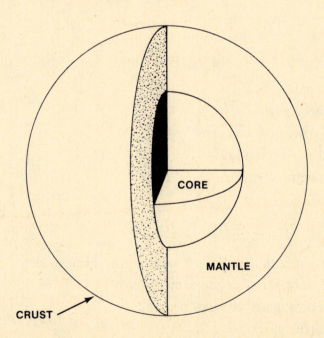

The thickness of the earth is about 8,000 miles. The crust is 20 to 30 miles thick. Beneath the crust is a thicker layer called the mantle. The mantle is about 1,800 miles thick. The rocky material that makes up the mantle is heavier and denser than the crust. Beneath the mantle, at the center of the earth, is the core. The core of the earth is very hot.

The earth is made up of many different parts. Earth science studies them all.

1.   This passage is mainly about

_____(1)   how big the earth is
_____(2)   the three different parts of the earth
_____(3)   how far the earth is from the sun
_____(4)   what science is
_____(5)   how much water is on our planet

2.   The hydrosphere is

_____(1)   the air that surrounds our planet
_____(2)   only the water in the ocean
_____(3)   almost half of our planet
_____(4)   all the water that is part of the earth
_____(5)   the crust of the earth

3.   The earth's land has three parts to it. The mantle is

_____(1)   the top part
_____(2)   the hottest part
_____(3)   the part beneath the crust
_____(4)   covered with mountains
_____(5)   at the center of the earth

4.   Oxygen and nitrogen

_____(1)   are the gases that make up most of the atmosphere
_____(2)   are the only gases in the atmosphere
_____(3)   are the only gases we can breathe
_____(4)   are colorful gases
_____(5)   cannot be mixed

5. If the atmosphere screened out too much sunlight,

_____(1)   the earth would dry up
_____(2)   the earth would be too cold for humans to live on it
_____(3)   the earth would have no water
_____(4)   the sun would get farther away from us
_____(5)   the earth would stop spinning

Answers start on page 81.

EARTH SCIENCES PASSAGE 2

> **KEY WORDS**
> **earthquake**—(noun) a shaking of the earth due to movements in the earth's crust
> **geologist**—(noun) a scientist who studies the earth

Have you ever felt an earthquake? An earthquake might be so small that you think that it is just the rumble of a truck driving past. Or it might be so strong that buildings fall down and the ground cracks. If you live in California, chances are you have felt many earthquakes. If you live in the Midwest you may have never felt the earth quake. In New Zealand there is an earthquake almost every day. Why is it that some places have so many earthquakes and some places have almost none?

Geologists are scientists who study the earth. In ancient times, people thought earthquakes were a sign that the gods were angry or that their king was going to die. Today, geologists know the real reason there are earthquakes.

The top layer of the earth is called the crust. The crust is 20 to 30 miles deep. Imagine that the crust of the earth is broken into different pieces. Imagine that six huge pieces and five smaller ones cover the entire earth. But they don't fit neatly together like pieces of a jigsaw puzzle. In some places they are too tight and rub against each other. In other places they overlap. Sometimes they are too loose and there is a crack between them.

Scientists call these pieces "plates." Tectonics is a word that means changes in the earth's crust. When geologists talk about earthquakes they will often talk about plate tectonics. Earthquakes happen when these plates move around. Almost all earthquakes happen where two plates come together. Scientists know where plates will move and, therefore, where earthquakes are likely to occur.

THE WORLD'S EARTHQUAKE ZONES —

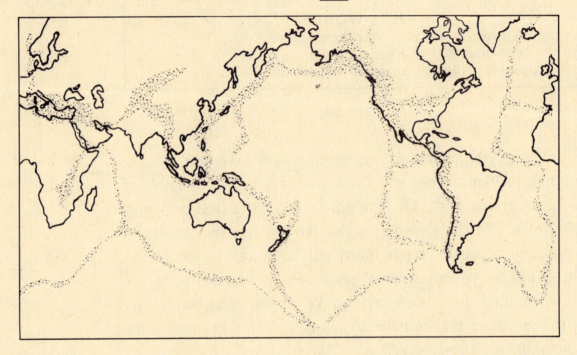

Seismographs are used to measure earthquakes. A seismograph is a very delicate machine that records movements in the ground. Seismograph readings let us look at the force of different earthquakes. The scale used is called the Richter scale. A very small earthquake will get a negative or minus reading on the Richter scale, just as a very cold day will get a negative reading on your thermometer.

The strongest recorded quakes have had readings of 8.9 on the Richter scale. An earthquake with a Richter number of more than 7 is usually serious. Even earthquakes that are 5 on the Richter scale may hurt buildings.

If you live in Australia or Africa or the middle of the United States, you don't need to worry much about earthquakes. But if you live in California or Alaska or Japan, be prepared for the plates to move!

6.   A good title for this passage would be

_____(1)   The Richter Scale
_____(2)   Seismographs
_____(3)   Geologists
_____(4)   Earthquakes
_____(5)   Tectonics

7.   The different pieces of the earth's crust are called

_____(1)   continents
_____(2)   geology
_____(3)   plates
_____(4)   tectonics
_____(5)   earthquakes

8.   When pieces of the earth move around,

_____(1)   there is a high reading on the Richter scale
_____(2)   there is a low reading on the Richter scale
_____(3)   a small or large earthquake may happen
_____(4)   geologists are puzzled
_____(5)   great storms may occur

9.   A reading of 8.0 on the Richter scale

_____(1)   means a very serious earthquake
_____(2)   doesn't mean anything
_____(3)   means the seismograph is broken
_____(4)   means a mild earthquake
_____(5)   means no one will be hurt

10.   From this passage we can tell that

_____(1)   geologists don't know much about earthquakes

_____(2)   seismographs do not work well

_____(3)   earthquakes are a sign that the gods are angry

_____(4)   earthquakes occur in all parts of the world

_____(5)   certain parts of the world are more dangerous to live in than others

Answers start on page 81.

EARTH SCIENCE PASSAGE 3

> **KEY WORD**
> **volcano**—(noun) a deep opening in the earth's crust where hot melted rock from inside the earth flows out and cools, forming a mountain

A recent <u>volcano</u> to erupt in the United States was Mount St. Helens in the state of Washington. When Mount St. Helens erupted, clouds of ash and smoke filled the air for days. In some towns miles away from the volcano, the streets were covered with ash four inches deep.

Volcanoes are like earthquakes in an important way. They both happen in the same parts of the world. Scientists know that the earth's crust is made of different pieces called plates. Where two plates join, the crust is weak. It is at these weak points that most earthquakes and volcanoes occur. Volcanoes are very likely where plates on the ocean floor meet plates that are under continents. One large plate was found under the Pacific Ocean. Where this Pacific plate meets the plates under America, Asia and Australia, there are many volcanoes. This is known as the circum-Pacific belt of fire.

A volcano begins as a deep opening in the earth's crust. The inside of the earth is much hotter than the crust. It is so hot that the rock will melt there. When it is inside the earth,

STRUCTURE AND PARTS OF A VOLCANO

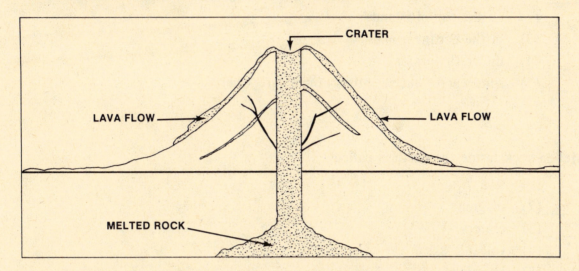

this rock is called magma. The magma will force its way up to the surface of the deep opening in the crust. When it reaches the surface, the magma is called lava. The lava flows out around the opening. As it cools, it becomes solid rock. As more lava flows out and cools a mountain is formed. The opening at the top of a volcano is called a crater. When a volcano erupts, steam, gas and ash are also given off.

A volcano may begin in the ocean floor. When the mountain is high enough the top of it will be an island. This is how the Hawaiian Islands were formed.

Volcanoes are often very harmful. Volcanic eruptions can wipe out whole towns, killing people and animals. But volcanoes have good points too. Volcanic ash makes very fertile soil. It adds rich minerals to the soil and this helps plants to grow there.

11.   This passage is mainly about

_____(1)   how volcanoes are like earthquakes

_____(2)   what lava is

_____(3)   what magma is

_____(4)   what volcanoes are and how they work

_____(5)   what is good about volcanoes

12. Most volcanoes and earthquakes occur

_____(1) at the weak point where two plates are joined

_____(2) on the top of islands

_____(3) in the ocean

_____(4) under the crater

_____(5) somewhere, but scientists aren't sure where

13. Melted rock inside the earth is called

_____(1) lava

_____(2) magma

_____(3) craters

_____(4) volcanic ash

_____(5) eruptions

14. Some mountains and islands are alike because

_____(1) neither one has volcanic ash nearby

_____(2) they are beautiful to look at

_____(3) they both may be the tops of volcanoes

_____(4) they are near each other

_____(5) they are in warm climates

15. Which of the following is *not* something we know about volcanoes?

_____(1) volcanoes are very powerful and destructive

_____(2) volcanic ash is good for the soil

_____(3) when lava cools, it turns to solid rock

_____(4) the Hawaiian Islands were formed from volcanoes

_____(5) scientists don't know what causes volcanoes

Answers start on page 81.

EARTH SCIENCE PASSAGE 4

┌───┐

KEY WORDS
ice age—(noun) a period of time when the earth's
    temperature drops and ice sheets cover much of
    the globe
interglacial—(noun) the time between ice ages

└───┘

Does it ever seem to you that the winters are getting colder? Or that summers aren't as hot as they used to be? It may not be happening yet, but sometime in the future the world will experience another ice age.

During an ice age the average temperature of the earth would drop by only five or ten degrees, but there would be big changes in the earth's climate. Ice sheets would cover much of the globe. Areas that are now good for farming would be too cold to grow crops. All of the northern United States would be under ice. Parts of Africa and South America that are now jungle would become grasslands. There would be less rainfall and more deserts.

Right now we are in an interglacial. This means we are in a period between ice ages. Most interglacials last about 12,000 years. This one has already lasted about 10,000 years. In fact, the temperature of the earth has been slowly dropping for the past 7,000 years. Scientists think that about 2,300 years from now we will be in the middle of the next ice age.

Ice ages happen because the earth sometimes moves slightly farther away from the sun. During these times the earth gets less heat from the sun and an ice age begins.

The last ice age began about 100,000 years ago and ended about 10,000 years ago. There are also little ice ages. These occur every 2,000 years. The last little ice age lasted from the year 1450 to the year 1850.

Some scientists think that the interglacial we are in now will be warmer and longer than most interglacials. This is because by burning coal and oil man has added carbon dioxide to the atmosphere. Carbon dioxide traps heat and so raises the temperature of the earth. If we keep burning coal and oil much longer, the earth will get so warm that some of the ice that covers the North and South Poles will melt. The water from the ice will raise the level of the oceans. This could cause problems for cities along the coasts.

It will be thousands of years before sheets of ice cover Chicago, New York and Denver, but some day it will happen. People in that time will have to live very differently from the way we do now.

16.   In this passage we learn

_____(1)   how to prepare for the coming ice age

_____(2)   what an ice age is

_____(3)   some of the problems cities along the ocean coasts will face soon

_____(4)   why there are changes in weather

_____(5)   how long a little ice age lasts

17.   Interglacials last about

_____(1)   12,000 years

_____(2)   10,000 years

_____(3)   7,000 years

_____(4)   400 years

_____(5)   100,000 years

18.   If we were alive during an ice age,

_____(1)   we would need to wear warmer clothes

_____(2)   we would never go swimming

_____(3)   our lives would change completely

_____(4)   we would all move south

_____(5)   it would be hard to grow flowers

19. How is man affecting the coming of the next ice age?

_____(1)   by building cities on the coasts
_____(2)   by fishing in the oceans
_____(3)   by learning to grow plants in colder temperatures
_____(4)   by adding carbon dioxide to the atmosphere, which raises the temperature of the earth
_____(5)   by learning how to keep the earth from moving away from the sun

20. Learning about ice ages might make us feel

_____(1)   what we do today doesn't matter
_____(2)   we can't control everything that happens to the earth
_____(3)   interglacials are boring times
_____(4)   our climate will never change
_____(5)   it won't make any difference when the next one comes

Answers start on page 81.

EARTH SCIENCE PASSAGE 5

KEY WORD
oil shale—(noun) a rock that turns into oil if it is buried beneath the earth for many years

There has been much talk in our country lately about the fuel shortage. Prices of gas and heating oil have gone up. Some scientists say the world will run out of oil by the year 2000.

The oil we are using today was formed millions of years ago. Oil was formed under oceans. Sometimes when an underwater plant died, it was covered with sand at the sea bottom. If all the ocean plants had been buried in sand, we would not have an oil shortage today. Most dead plants simply decayed and became part of the ocean floor. Plants and animals usually decay this way because of the oxygen in the water. The few dead plants that were buried in sand were not exposed to oxygen, so they did not decay in the usual way. Instead, after millions of years, these plants turned into a rock called oil shale. In some cases the oil shale moved deeper into the earth where it is hotter. This is the oil shale that became oil.

Coal was formed much the same way oil was, except coal was formed on land from trees. Some trees fell in swamps where there is little oxygen in the water. After being buried for millions of years, this wood became coal. Today there is much more coal left in the ground than oil. We might have enough coal to last for another 100 years.

Oil and coal are both formed very slowly. It took millions of years to make the oil and coal we have used up in

TYPES OF ENERGY USED IN THE UNITED STATES

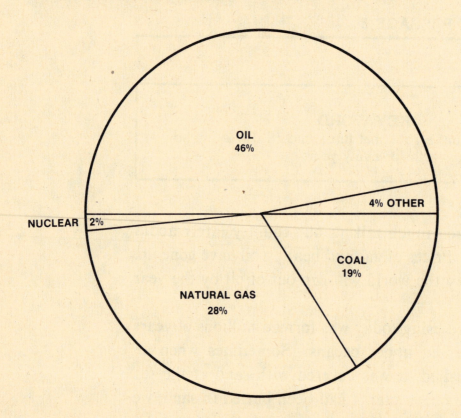

the last 100 years. We are using these fuels much, much faster than they are being formed. Oil and coal are called non-renewable resources. When they are gone, we will never have them again. Wood is a renewable resource. If you cut down a tree, you can plant a new one. Solar energy is also a renewable resource because sunlight is never used up.

Looking at the figure you can see that most of the energy we use today comes from oil, coal and natural gas. These are all non-renewable fuels. Hopefully, we will learn more about how to use renewable fuels.

21. A good title for this passage would be

_____(1) How Oil Is Formed
_____(2) Our Energy Problems
_____(3) Where Coal Comes From
_____(4) The Story of Oil and Coal
_____(5) Using Solar Energy

22. Coal is formed

_____(1) from dead plants and animals
_____(2) from wood that has been buried for millions of years
_____(3) from solar energy
_____(4) from renewable fuels
_____(5) in new batches every few years

23. Oil is formed

_____(1) from underwater plants buried in the sand without oxygen for millions of years
_____(2) from dead trees
_____(3) from the heat of the sun
_____(4) from old coal
_____(5) very quickly

24. If we are not careful about how we use coal and oil,

_____(1)   we will get burned

_____(2)   we will freeze

_____(3)   they will be used up before we have found something
else to use in their place

_____(4)   they will spill all over the land and oceans

_____(5)   they will dirty our air

25. After reading this passage we might want to

_____(1)   learn how we can use more wood and solar energy as
fuel

_____(2)   find out where there is more oil

_____(3)   find out how to change oil shale into oil

_____(4)   find some trees that have been buried for millions of
years

_____(5)   give up and learn to live without fuel

Answers start on page 82.

EARTH SCIENCE PASSAGE 6

KEY WORDS

air pollution—(noun) smoke, gases and particles that
make the air dirty

water pollution—(noun) waste from factories or sewage
systems that makes the water dirty

On TV news in some cities there is something new in the
weather report. The weatherman predicts how bad the air
pollution will be the next day. This report is very important
for elderly people, people who have bad hearts and people
who have lung diseases. If the air pollution is bad, these
people should stay indoors and not do any hard work. Even
for healthy people, air pollution is unpleasant. Years of
living where the air is very polluted may cause people to get
lung diseases, such as emphysema, or even cancer.

Most air pollution is caused by burning oil or coal.

When these fuels burn they do not burn completely. They leave smoke, gases and small particles that fill the air. Natural gas is a clean fuel. It burns completely so that no smoke or dust is left. There are two main sources of air pollution: factories and cars.

Nuclear power doesn't pollute the air, but it leaves wastes that must be buried underground. This can be a source of water pollution. If buried wastes from nuclear plants or other factories seep out of their storage containers, the wastes will get into rivers and lakes. The worst case of pollution from buried wastes happened at Love Canal. Love Canal is part of the city of Niagara Falls in New York. From the 1930s until 1953 the Hooker Chemical Company buried its wastes at Love Canal. Hooker is a company that makes pesticides—to kill insects—plastics and other chemicals. During the 1970s people who lived near the chemical dump saw the trees and grass in their yards die. Strange black or red liquids would seep into their basements and up into their lawns. Many people got liver and kidney diseases. Some people got cancer. Many children were born with birth defects. In 1979, the government paid for the people nearest the dump to move because the area was so dangerous.

Water also gets polluted because some factories and sewage systems dump wastes directly into lakes, rivers or oceans. Beaches are often closed to swimmers because of this kind of pollution.

Clean air and water are important for our health and safety. In the future maybe we will find cleaner fuels and better ways to dispose of wastes.

26. This passage tells about

    _____(1)   Love Canal
    _____(2)   nuclear power
    _____(3)   the Hooker Chemical Company
    _____(4)   weather reports
    _____(5)   different types of pollution

27.   Most air pollution is caused by

_____(1)   nuclear wastes

_____(2)   sewage

_____(3)   burning oil or coal

_____(4)   chemical wastes

_____(5)   strange black or red liquids

28.   People who live close to places where dangerous chemicals are dumped

_____(1)   could become seriously ill

_____(2)   will not like the way the air smells

_____(3)   are perfectly safe

_____(4)   complain a lot

_____(5)   can't have children

29.   Natural gas is called a clean fuel because

_____(1)   it cleans the air as it burns

_____(2)   it has no odor

_____(3)   it burns completely leaving no smoke or dust

_____(4)   it really isn't clean

_____(5)   it doesn't pollute water

30.   The passage doesn't say so, but it is probably true that

_____(1)   some day we will not be able to go swimming

_____(2)   scientists are working on ways to find cleaner fuels

_____(3)   the Hooker Chemical Company is going out of business

_____(4)   no one wants to visit Niagara Falls

_____(5)   air pollution isn't that dangerous

Answers start on page 82.

EARTH SCIENCE PASSAGE 7

> ### KEY WORDS
> **passive solar heating—**(noun) a way of heating buildings
> with sunlight that uses no equipment except the
> building itself

Most people heat their homes with natural gas, oil or electricity. A few people are using the sun to heat their homes. Heat from the sun is free, plentiful and it won't cause air pollution. Building or remodeling a house to use solar energy can be expensive. But since there are no fuel costs, a house with solar heat will be much cheaper in the long run.

If your house is in a place that is very sunny or where it doesn't get very cold in the winter, you might be able to use only solar heating. If you live where it is often cloudy or where the winters are very cold, you might need a furnace to use some of the time.

PASSIVE SOLAR HEATING

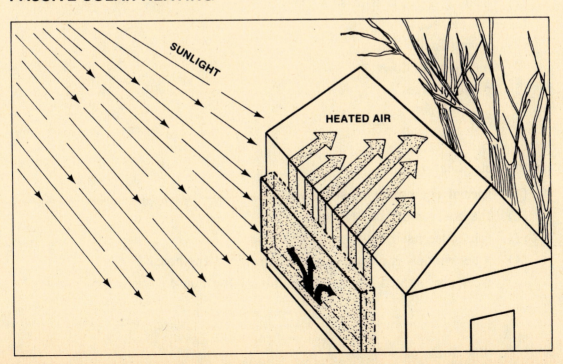

In some kinds of solar heating no special equipment is used. This is called <u>passive solar heating</u>. The house itself is used to catch the sun's heat. This is how a passive solar heating system works: The south side of the house is usually the sunniest. A huge window is built on this side of the house. The window has two layers of glass with a space of one or two feet in between. There is an open space running all the way around the house as shown in the diagram. Hot air is lighter than cold air, so it rises. The air between the windows is heated by the sun and then rises to the attic. As the air cools, it falls down the north side of the house to the crawl space under the house and then comes around to the big window where it is warmed again. The cold north side of the house is built with no windows. A row of trees might be planted on this side to break the wind. The entire house is very well insulated.

Solar energy is a new, exciting way to heat homes. Almost everywhere solar energy can help save oil and money.

31. This passage is mainly about

_____(1)   heating a house with solar energy
_____(2)   saving money
_____(3)   saving fuel
_____(4)   building windows
_____(5)   planting trees

32. In passive solar heating

_____(1)   special equipment must be used
_____(2)   the house must be very old
_____(3)   the house itself catches the sun's heat
_____(4)   a big window is placed on the north side of the house
_____(5)   trees are planted on the south side of the house

33. The fact that hot air rises

_____(1) causes the air to move around the inside of the house and be heated over and over again
_____(2) makes passive solar heating a poor system
_____(3) means you shouldn't have an attic
_____(4) makes people too warm
_____(5) can be changed if you plant trees in the right place

34. Which is *not* a good reason for using solar heating?

_____(1) heat from the sun is free
_____(2) solar heat doesn't cause air pollution
_____(3) we will never run out of solar energy
_____(4) the large window is too expensive
_____(5) though it's expensive at first, it's cheaper in the long run

35. In the future we will probably

_____(1) find more natural gas and oil
_____(2) make electricity cheaper
_____(3) use more solar energy
_____(4) learn to live with pollution
_____(5) find that solar energy becomes more expensive

Answers start on page 82.

EARTH SCIENCE PASSAGE 8

KEY WORDS

core—(noun) the center of the sun
photosphere—(noun) the layer of the sun that surrounds the core
chromosphere—(noun) the third layer out from the center of the sun
corona—(noun) the pale outer layer of the sun

Did you know that the sun is a star much like the stars you see twinkling in the night sky? The sun looks so much bigger and brighter because it is so much closer to the earth. The sun is 93 million miles from Earth. The next closest star is 21 trillion miles away.

The sun is about five billion years old. It is a middle-aged star. Scientists think the sun will last for another five billion years. As stars go, the sun is about average in its size and temperature. Some stars are much larger than the sun and others are much smaller. Also there are stars that are much hotter than the sun and stars that are much cooler.

When the sun first formed, it was very cool—only about 5,000° Fahrenheit. It took a half billion years for the sun to heat up to its present temperature.

The sun is not solid like the earth. It is all gas. But the gas of the sun is in four layers. The core or center of the sun is the hottest part. Its temperature is about 29,000,000° F. This is where the heat of the sun is made. The way the sun makes heat is very complicated. It is a little bit like millions of atomic bombs exploding. The heat from the sun's core works its way up to another layer called the photosphere.

LAYERS OF THE SUN

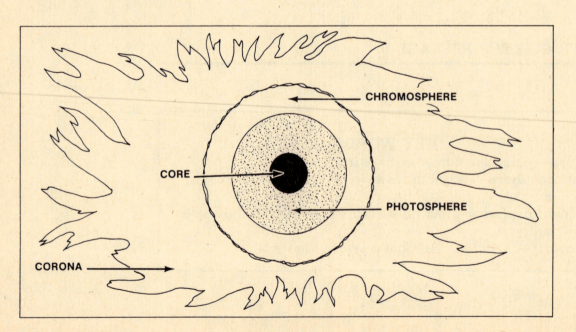

The photosphere is much cooler than the core. Its temperature is about 10,000° F. The photosphere is what we see when we look at the sun.

Outside the photosphere is the chromosphere. In the chromosphere the temperature rises again to about 25,000° F. Imagine the photosphere as an ocean that is very rough with high waves. The chromosphere is like the spray of water in the air from the photosphere. The outermost layer of the sun is the corona. The corona extends for a million miles around the sun, but it can't be seen from the earth. It is too pale.

When the sun dies, our whole solar system will die with it. When it gets very old, the sun will expand. It will be 100 times bigger than it is today. The earth and all the other planets will be burned up. Still later, the sun will shrink and cool until it is only a black clump of carbon.

The sun is a fascinating star. Without it there would be no life on Earth. But don't stare at the sun too long. Even though it is only an average star, the sun is bright enough to blind you!

36. This passage tells mostly

_____(1)   about the photosphere and the chromosphere
_____(2)   how the solar system will die
_____(3)   about stars that are bigger than the sun
_____(4)   not to stare at the sun
_____(5)   all about the sun and its different parts

37. The temperature at the core of the sun is

_____(1)   10,000° F.
_____(2)   29,000,000° F.
_____(3)   25,000° F.
_____(4)   5,000° F.
_____(5)   93,000° F.

38.   Heat is made in the sun's core by a process

_____(1)   that is like coal burning

_____(2)   that is like oil burning

_____(3)   that is like millions of atomic bombs exploding

_____(4)   that is like dynamite exploding

_____(5)   that scientists don't understand

39.   Some day the solar system will die because

_____(1)   the sun will expand when it gets very old and burn up the planets

_____(2)   the sun will get cold and the planets will freeze

_____(3)   it will get too old

_____(4)   the sun will move away from it

_____(5)   the planets will spin out away from the sun

40.   We can tell from this passage that

_____(1)   the sun will burn out soon

_____(2)   we see the chromosphere when we look at the sun

_____(3)   the earth is totally dependent on the sun

_____(4)   the sun is hotter on the outside than the inside

_____(5)   nobody knows what the corona is

Answers start on page 82.

EARTH SCIENCE PASSAGE 9

KEY WORDS

solar system—(noun) a star and the planets that surround it

No one has ever seen a planet besides the ones that move around our sun. Just by looking into the sky you can see hundreds of stars. Scientists with powerful telescopes can see millions more. Yet no telescope is powerful enough to see the planets surrounding another star. Scientists think that other stars have planets too, because all stars are formed in much the same way and planets are formed with them.

There are nine planets in our <u>solar system</u>. Mercury is the planet closest to the sun. After Mercury come Venus, Earth and Mars. These planets are all very dense. They are made of heavy rocks and metals. Earth is the largest of these four planets; Venus is a little smaller than Earth. Mercury and Mars are about half the size of Earth. You can find a picture of the solar system in Physics Passage 3 on page 113. This diagram compares the sizes of the nine planets.

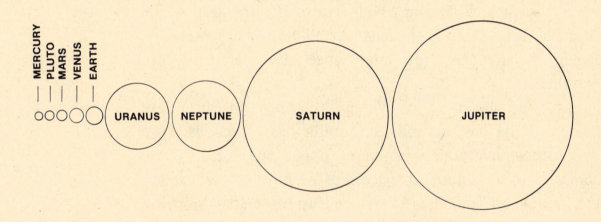

Mercury is the smallest planet in the solar system. From the outside, Mercury looks like our moon. It is covered with water. But our moon is made of very light rock. On the inside, Mercury is made of heavy metal and rock like the Earth. Mercury has no atmosphere or air around it.

Venus has a surface temperature of about 800° Fahrenheit. It is the hottest planet. Venus is this hot because it has a thick atmosphere of carbon dioxide. This traps heat. The atmosphere on Venus is so thick that standing on the surface of the planet would be like standing under 33 feet of water here on Earth.

Mars has a very thin atmosphere of carbon dioxide. Today temperatures on Mars range from $-120°$ F. at night to $-20°$ F. during the day. Mars may have been warmer in the past. Markings on the planet's surface suggest that water once flowed there.

The next planets out from the sun are Jupiter, Saturn, Uranus and Neptune. These planets are much lighter than the first four and much larger. Instead of being solid, they are balls of gas. Jupiter is by far the biggest planet. Less is known about these planets than about the four planets closest to the sun. All four of these large planets have thick atmospheres. Huge storms can be seen on Jupiter and Saturn.

Very little is known about Pluto, the farthest planet from the sun. Pluto is the smallest planet besides Mercury. Scientists think that Pluto might once have been a moon of Neptune.

All the planets except Venus, Mercury and Pluto have moons. Mars has two moons. Jupiter has 14 moons.

Almost everything we know about our solar system comes from satellites and spaceships we have sent to explore the planets and moons. As we send up more spaceships we will learn more and more about our solar system.

41.   A good title for this passage would be

_____(1)   How a Star Gets Planets
_____(2)   How the Earth Revolves around the Sun
_____(3)   Life on Mars
_____(4)   Our Solar System
_____(5)   Space Travel

42. Venus is very hot because

_____(1) it is the closest planet to the sun

_____(2) it has a thick atmosphere of carbon dioxide, which traps heat

_____(3) it is so small it warms up quickly

_____(4) it has no clouds so that it gets more sun

_____(5) it has too much water, which holds in the heat

43. Jupiter and Saturn are

_____(1) lighter and larger than the planets closer to the sun

_____(2) small planets

_____(3) planets that may have life on them

_____(4) the planets that we know most about

_____(5) the hottest planets

44. Since we are learning about our solar system from satellites and spaceships,

_____(1) we'll never learn anything else

_____(2) it costs too much to learn more and money is needed elsewhere

_____(3) we will need to make our space program grow in order to learn more

_____(4) nobody wants to know any more because there are enough problems on Earth

_____(5) we won't learn anything because scientists can't travel in spaceships

45. Although we can't see them, there are probably planets around other stars. This means that

_____(1) there may be life on other planets outside our solar system

_____(2) there couldn't possibly be life on other planets

_____(3) these planets may crash into our solar system

_____(4) these other solar systems would be exactly the same as ours

_____(5) we will never find these planets

Answers start on page 82.

EARTH SCIENCE PASSAGE 10

> **KEY WORDS**
> **astronomer**—(noun) a scientist who studies the stars and other planets
> **space probe**—(noun) an unmanned spaceship that sends back pictures to Earth

Saturn is the sixth planet from the sun. It is more than 900 million miles away from the Earth. Saturn is the second largest planet in our solar system. Only Jupiter is larger. Saturn is 755 times larger than the Earth. But Saturn is also a very light planet. It weighs only 95 times as much as Earth. Saturn may have a small core of metal, but mostly the planet is just gases. Saturn is covered by an ocean of liquid hydrogen. On Earth, hydrogen is usually a gas. Hydrogen can exist as a liquid on Saturn, because the planet is very cold.

Even from Earth astronomers can see that there are rings around Saturn. In fact, they can see three rings.

In 1980 an unmanned space probe called Voyager I flew by Saturn and took the first close-up pictures. These pictures were beamed back to Earth where they were studied by astronomers.

There were many surprises in the Voyager I pictures of Saturn. Instead of three large rings, Saturn has hundreds of tiny rings. These rings are like the grooves on a record. The particles of dust that make up the rings are very small. A spaceship can fly through the rings without being hurt. The most surprising discovery the scientists made was that one of the rings is really three strands braided together. Scientists are not able to say why the braid doesn't fall apart as it circles Saturn. Scientists don't know why some planets have rings. In our solar system Jupiter and Uranus also have small rings.

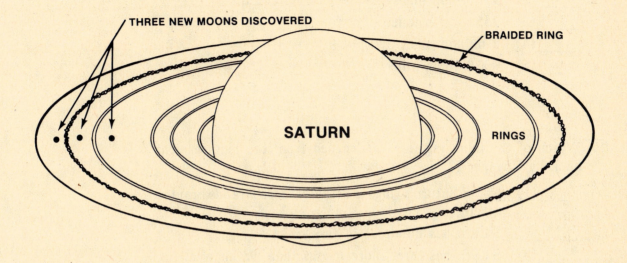

THREE NEW MOONS DISCOVERED

BRAIDED RING

SATURN

RINGS

Voyager I also discovered three new moons of Saturn. These were the 12th, 13th and 14th moons to be found. One of the old moons, Titan, was found to have an atmosphere made of nitrogen. This may give a clue as to what the Earth's atmosphere was like when our planet was first formed.

It took Voyager I more than three years to get near Saturn. On its way to Saturn, Voyager sent back pictures of Mars and Jupiter. Now Voyager I will go out of our solar system. Voyager I carries a picture of a man and a woman and of Earth, so that if a traveler from another solar system finds it, he or she will know where Voyager I came from.

Voyager I sent back exciting new pictures of Saturn. By 1981 another space probe, Voyager II, will have visited Saturn. With each new visit our knowledge of Saturn grows.

46. This passage could be called
_____(1) Saturn and Jupiter
_____(2) The Discoveries of Voyager I
_____(3) All about Space Travel
_____(4) Taking Pictures in Space
_____(5) The Coming of Voyager II

47.   The distance of Saturn from the earth is

      (1)   93 million miles

      (2)   95 million miles

      (3)   755 million miles

      (4)   2 million miles

      (5)   900 million miles

48.   Which of the following was *not* learned from the pictures sent back by Voyager I?

      (1)   one of Saturn's rings is actually three strands braided together

      (2)   Saturn has hundreds of tiny rings

      (3)   Saturn has three more moons than we knew about

      (4)   Saturn has rings around it

      (5)   one of Saturn's moons has an atmosphere made of nitrogen

49.   Voyager I will be going next

      (1)   out of the solar system

      (2)   back to Mars

      (3)   back to Earth

      (4)   straight to the sun

      (5)   to land on one of Saturn's moons

50.   From this passage we can guess that

      (1)   we will never understand the solar system

      (2)   scientists are looking forward to learning more about Saturn in the future

      (3)   Saturn's rings are dangerous to spaceships

      (4)   Voyager II will never get off the ground

      (5)   Voyager II will not beam pictures back to Earth

Answers start on page 83.

ANSWERS AND EXPLANATIONS—EARTH SCIENCE

1. **(2)** is the correct answer. It is the main idea of the passage. (1), (4) and (5) are touched on briefly and (3) is not mentioned at all.

2. **(4)** is correct. All the others are false.

3. **(3)** is correct. All others are false.

4. **(1)** is correct. All the others are false.

5. **(2)** is correct. The passage tells us that if the atmosphere did not screen out some sunlight the earth would be a lifeless desert. From this we can conclude that if the atmosphere screened out too much sunlight it would be too cold.

6. **(4)** is the correct answer. All the others are mentioned in the passage but are not the main idea.

7. **(3)** is correct. All the others are false.

8. **(3)** is correct. Movement of plates causes earthquakes. Some movements cause large quakes and some cause small quakes.

9. **(1)** is correct. The passage says that any reading of more than 7 is usually serious.

10. **(5)** is correct. The passage names, in the first paragraph and in the last, several places that have many earthquakes. It also names some places that almost never have earthquakes.

11. **(4)** is the correct answer. All the others are just *parts* of what is discussed in the passage.

12. **(1)** is correct. All the others are false.

13. **(2)** is correct. All the others are false.

14. **(3)** is correct. The passage explains that a volcano forms a mountain around it. If this happens in the ocean, the top of that mountain looks like an island to us.

15. **(5)** is the right answer. From everything the passage tells us about volcanoes, we can conclude that scientists *do* know what causes them.

16. **(2)** is correct. It best sums up what the passage is about.

17. **(1)** is correct.

18. **(3)** is correct. It best sums up the effect on us of all the things the passage says would happen in an ice age.

19. **(4)** is correct.

20. **(2)** is correct. All the others are false.

21. **(4)** is correct. The others are mentioned in the passage, but none is the main idea.

22. **(2)** is correct. All the others are false.

23. **(1)** is correct. All the others are false.

24. **(3)** is correct. The author tells us that oil and coal are nonrenewable and that we are using them up very fast.

25. **(1)** is correct. The passage suggests that the only hope is in finding out how to use renewable fuels.

26. **(5)** is the main idea. The others are all mentioned but are not the main idea of the passage.

27. **(3)** is correct.

28. **(1)** is correct. The passage gives an example of a place where this has happened.

29. **(3)** is the correct answer.

30. **(2)** is correct. The passage tells us how bad pollution is and says that we must find cleaner fuels.

31. **(1)** is the main idea. The other points are mentioned in some way, but are not the main idea.

32. **(3)** is correct. All the others are false.

33. **(1)** is correct. The passage explains how the rising of hot air makes a passive solar heating system work.

34. **(4)** is the correct answer. All the others are covered in the passage as good reasons for using solar energy.

35. **(3)** is correct. The passage suggests in several places that solar energy is the best solution to our oil and money problems.

36. **(5)** is correct. The others are mentioned, but are not the main idea of the passage.

37. **(2)** is correct.

38. **(3)** is correct. All the others are false.

39. **(1)** is correct. Before it gets cold, the sun will get bigger and burn up the planets.

40. **(3)** is the only conclusion we can come to after reading this passage.

41. **(4)** is the best answer. This passage tells about all the planets in our solar system.

42. **(2)** is the correct answer. All the others are false.

43. **(1)** is correct. All the others are false.

44. **(3)** is the correct answer.

45. **(1)** is the correct conclusion to come to.

46. **(2)** would be the best title.

47. **(5)** is correct.

48. **(4)** was not discovered by Voyager I. We already knew that Saturn has rings.

49. **(1)** is correct. All the others are false.

50. **(2)** is correct. The passage tells us that Voyager II will visit Saturn.

UNIT III: CHEMISTRY

Chemistry is the study of matter—its makeup, structure and properties.

Directions: Read each passage. As you read, think about the ideas, facts and examples given. Study any pictures or charts that go with the passages. The Key Words will give you an idea of what the passage is about. They are used in the passage along with other new words. Look up any word that is new in the Glossary at the end of the book. You will be able to figure out many new words as you read them in the passage.

After each passage, there are five questions for you to answer. Each question builds a reading skill. Make a check mark (✔) next to the BEST answer for each question.

The Answers and Explanations begin on page 104.

CHEMISTRY PASSAGE 1

> ### KEY WORDS
> **matter**—(noun) anything that has a size and weight
> **element**—(noun) matter in its most basic form
> **compound**—(noun) two or more elements combined to form a new substance
> **atom**—(noun) the smallest part that makes up matter

How many of the things that you do in a day do you think have something to do with chemistry? Almost everything you do is part of chemistry. When you boil water for your morning coffee, that is chemistry. If you stir sugar into your coffee, that is chemistry, too. When you cook an egg, you are doing chemistry. If you find your car battery dead, you may be upset, but you are learning about chemistry. Breathing, eating, thinking and sleeping all involve many different chemicals inside your body.

Chemistry is the study of matter. It is easy to say what matter is. Everything that has a size and weight is matter. A tiny speck of dust, a mountain and a pet dog are all made of matter. Chemistry studies what matter is made of, the different kinds of matter and how matter is put together. The scientists who study matter are called chemists.

The ancient Greeks were the first people to think about what matter is. In a way, they were the first chemists. Some of the Greeks thought that all matter was made of earth, air, fire and water. They thought earth, air, fire and water were the four elements. An element is matter in its most basic form. It cannot be broken down any more. Any way you divide up an element, you will still have that element. A compound is two or more elements combined.

Today, chemists know there are 106 different elements. Oxygen is an element, so is hydrogen. These two elements combine to make the compound water. Gold and silver are elements. Mercury, the silver colored liquid inside thermometers, is an element. Helium is the element used to fill balloons so they will rise up in the air and float. Salt is a compound made of the elements sodium and chlorine. Both compounds and elements can be called chemicals.

The ancient Greeks thought that earth, air, fire and water were the basic building blocks of the world. Today chemists know that atoms are the basic building blocks from which everything is made. An atom is smaller than anyone can see. For an atom to be seen, it would have to be enlarged millions of times. An element is made of just one kind of atom. Each of the 106 elements on Earth is made of a different kind of atom. Compounds are made of two or more different kinds of atom.

When chemists talk about the world they talk about atoms, elements, compounds and chemicals. You may think stirring sugar into your coffee is just a simple, everyday thing to do. But it is also part of the world of chemistry.

1. The main idea of this passage is

_____(1)   chemistry is the study of different kinds of matter

_____(2)   the ancient Greeks

_____(3)   atoms, elements and compounds

_____(4)   everyday chemistry experiments

_____(5)   sodium and chlorine

2. An element is

_____(1)   the same thing as a compound

_____(2)   the same thing as an atom

_____(3)   made up of only one kind of atom

_____(4)   earth, air, fire or water

_____(5)   a substance like water or salt

3. A compound

_____(1)   can't be divided into elements

_____(2)   can be divided into two or more elements

_____(3)   always floats

_____(4)   is a substance like gold or silver

_____(5)   is a basic building block of the world

4. An atom is

_____(1)   like a lump of mercury

_____(2)   another word for matter

_____(3)   always very large

_____(4)   smaller than anyone can see

_____(5)   made of compounds

5.   After reading this passage, you can conclude that

_____(1)   chemistry is only done in laboratories

_____(2)   chemistry only involves atoms

_____(3)   chemistry only involves elements

_____(4)   chemistry only involves compounds

_____(5)   chemistry is a part of everyday life

Answers start on page 104.

CHEMISTRY PASSAGE 2

KEY WORDS

proton—(noun) one of the three parts of an atom; protons are found in the center of an atom in the nucleus

neutron—(noun) one of the three parts of an atom; neutrons are found in the center of the atom

electron—(noun) one of the three parts of an atom; electrons orbit the center of the atom

---

Matter is everything that has size and weight. A feather is matter, but things like your thoughts are not. The smallest part that matter can be broken down into is called an atom. There is a different type of atom for each element found on Earth. A hydrogen atom is different from a sodium atom. Each of these is different from an atom of silver.

An atom is made of at least three kinds of particles. These three particles are protons, neutrons and electrons. Chemists are now working to see if there are any other kinds of particles. Protons and neutrons are about the same size. They are each much bigger than an electron. A proton or a neutron is almost 2,000 times larger than an electron. The center of an atom is called the nucleus. The protons and neutrons of an atom make up the nucleus. The electrons fly around the nucleus much the same way planets move around the sun in our solar system. The path of a planet around the sun is called its orbit. The path of an electron around the nucleus is also called its orbit.

Most of the time atoms have the same number of protons and electrons. Carbon has six protons and six electrons. Iron has 26 protons and 26 electrons. Usually an atom has the same number of neutrons as of protons and electrons, but this is not always true. Hydrogen has one proton and one electron, but it has no neutrons. Helium has two protons, two electrons and two neutrons.

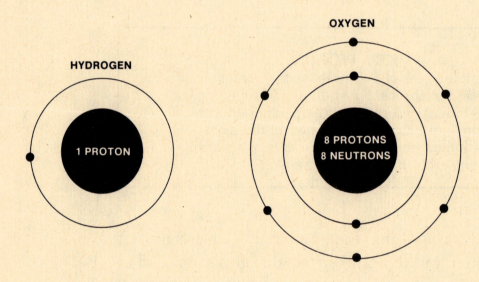

Chemists talk about elements in terms of their atomic number and atomic weight. The atomic number of an element is the number of protons in an atom of that element. Usually this is also the number of electrons in the element. Sometimes it is also the number of neutrons. Hydrogen has the atomic number "one." The atomic number of oxygen is "eight." Oxygen has eight protons, eight electrons and eight neutrons. The atomic number of sodium is "eleven." Sodium has 11 protons, 11 electrons and 12 neutrons.

Chemists give an atomic weight of "one" to each of the protons and neutrons of carbon. The protons of other elements weigh a little more or a little less than the protons of carbon. So the atomic weight of the protons of other elements is close to one but not exactly one. The atomic weight of carbon is 12.011. The six protons and six neutrons of carbon together weigh 12. The six electrons together weigh .011. The following chart gives the atomic number and atomic weight of several important elements.

ELEMENT	ATOMIC NUMBER	ATOMIC WEIGHT
Hydrogen	1	1.008
Carbon	6	12.011
Oxygen	8	16.000
Sodium	11	22.997
Aluminum	12	26.992
Iron	26	55.85
Silver	47	107.88
Gold	79	197.0

Although they are too small to see, everything in the world is made of atoms. Not only are the atoms too small to see, but they are made up of parts that are even smaller. These parts are protons, neutrons and electrons. It is because there are many different kinds of atoms that things in the world look, feel, taste and smell different.

6. The main idea of this passage is to explain

_____(1) the nucleus of the atom

_____(2) atomic weight

_____(3) atomic number

_____(4) what particles are in the atom

_____(5) the orbit of the electron

7. The nucleus of an atom contains

_____(1)   electrons

_____(2)   protons and neutrons

_____(3)   orbits

_____(4)   more atoms

_____(5)   helium

8. As the number of protons grows in different elements, their atomic numbers are

_____(1)   larger

_____(2)   smaller

_____(3)   the same

_____(4)   larger or smaller

_____(5)   the same as the atomic weight

9. Atomic weight is based on the weight of

_____(1)   the protons of oxygen

_____(2)   the neutrons of helium

_____(3)   the protons and neutrons of carbon

_____(4)   the electrons of hydrogen

_____(5)   the use of an atomic scale

10. After reading this passage, you can conclude that

_____(1)   atoms have only a nucleus

_____(2)   atoms have only protons and electrons

_____(3)   atoms have only protons and neutrons

_____(4)   atoms have a nucleus of protons and neutrons and orbits of electrons

_____(5)   atoms have only protons

Answers start on page 104.

CHEMISTRY PASSAGE 3

> ### KEY WORD
> **molecule**—(noun) two or more atoms attached together

Everything that has size and weight is matter. All matter is made of atoms. Atoms are tiny particles. The parts of an atom are protons, neutrons and electrons. The protons and neutrons of an atom make up its nucleus. The atom's electrons move around the nucleus the way the earth moves around the sun.

A molecule is two or more atoms linked together. The atoms that make up a molecule might be atoms of the same element or of different elements. The oxygen in the air we breathe is in molecules of two oxygen atoms. Water is a molecule made of three atoms. The atoms in water are two hydrogen atoms and one oxygen atom.

You may be wondering how atoms stick together to make a molecule. This has to do with the way the electrons are arranged in atoms. The electrons that fly around the nucleus of an atom are arranged in layers or levels. These levels are called shells. Each shell can hold a certain number of electrons and no more. The first shell of an atom is the one closest to the nucleus. The first shell can hold two electrons. Hydrogen has one electron. That one electron is in the first shell. Helium has two electrons. The first shell of helium is completely filled with its two electrons. Lithium is the element that has three electrons. Lithium's first two electrons fill up the first shell. Its third electron goes into the second shell. The second shell can hold up to eight electrons. Carbon has six electrons. Its first two electrons go into the first shell. The other four go into the second shell. The

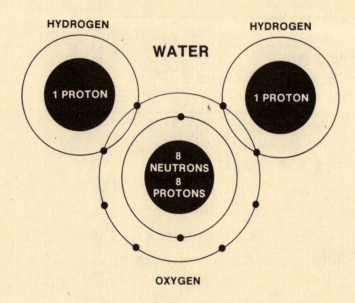

second shell of carbon isn't completely filled because it has only four electrons.

Although atoms don't have thoughts or feelings, you might say that an atom "wants" its last shell to be full. A hydrogen atom has only one electron. It would "like to have" two electrons so its first shell would be full. Suppose two hydrogen atoms were to join and share their electrons. The two electrons would move around both nuclei. This way both atoms would have two electrons, and two electrons are a full first shell. Oxygen has eight electrons, two in the first shell and six in the second shell. If oxygen had two more electrons its second shell would be full. So oxygen joins with two hydrogen atoms to make water.

When water and hydrogen molecules form, the atoms share electrons. In other cases, one atom takes an electron away from another atom. This is what happens when salt is formed. The salt we put on our food is made of two elements: sodium and chlorine. Sodium has 11 electrons. There are two electrons in sodium's first shell, eight in its second shell and one in its third shell. Chlorine has 17 electrons: two in the first shell, eight in the second shell and seven in the third shell. The chlorine atom takes away the one electron in the third shell of sodium. This way chlorine has a full third shell of eight electrons. By losing its one electron in the third shell, sodium has a full second shell with no electrons left over.

Every atom would like to have a full electron shell. When atoms join to make molecules, they get their full shells by sharing electrons with other atoms, by taking electrons from other atoms or by losing electrons to other atoms.

11. The main idea of this passage is
_____(1)   how atoms are made
_____(2)   how molecules are made
_____(3)   how electrons move
_____(4)   how water is formed
_____(5)   how a nucleus is made

12. The number of electrons in the first three shells is
_____(1)   eight, eight, two
_____(2)   two, eight, two
_____(3)   two, eight, eight
_____(4)   eight, two, two
_____(5)   two, two, eight

13. Different atoms combine to make molecules with
_____(1)   shared or moved electrons
_____(2)   shared or moved protons
_____(3)   shared or moved neutrons
_____(4)   shared nuclei
_____(5)   shared electrons and protons

14. When salt is formed,
_____(1)   sodium takes an electron from chlorine
_____(2)   chlorine takes a proton from chlorine
_____(3)   sodium takes a proton from chlorine
_____(4)   chlorine takes an electron from sodium
_____(5)   chlorine takes a neutron from sodium

15.   After reading this passage, you can conclude that

_____(1)   electron shells are never full in any molecules

_____(2)   electron shells "want" to be full when molecules are formed

_____(3)   electron shells are always full when molecules are formed

_____(4)   electron shells are the same in all atoms and molecules

_____(5)   electron shells do not change when molecules are formed

Answers start on page 104.

CHEMISTRY PASSAGE 4

KEY WORDS

chemical formula—(noun) a short way of showing a chemical reaction

chemical reaction—(noun) atoms or molecules combining to make new molecules

product—(noun) the new molecules that are made in a chemical reaction

reactant—(noun) the atoms or molecules that combine and change in a chemical reaction

---

To a chemist the world is made up of atoms. These atoms may be alone, or they may be combined with other atoms to make molecules. A molecule can be very simple. It can have only two or three atoms. Or a molecule can be large and complicated. A single molecule can have as many as 10,000 atoms. Molecules of compounds inside our bodies are often very large. Proteins, which are a type of compound, are among the largest molecules. The life of a chemist would be very difficult if he had to list every atom in a 10,000 atom molecule. To make their work easier, chemists use a shortcut to write and talk about atoms and molecules. They use chemical formulas to talk about how atoms combine. What would take pages to tell in words can sometimes be said in a few lines of formulas.

To begin with, chemists use one or two letters to stand for each of the 106 elements. The letter for hydrogen is H. The letter for oxygen is O. The letters for sodium are Na. The chart that follows lists the chemical symbols (letters) of some important elements.

ELEMENT	SYMBOL
Hydrogen	H
Carbon	C
Oxygen	O
Sodium	Na
Aluminum	Al
Iron	Fe
Silver	Ag
Gold	Au

The addition sign (+) is used to show that two atoms or molecules combine. An arrow points to the molecule that is formed by the atoms joining. The formula

$$H_2 + O \rightarrow H_2O$$

shows that two atoms of hydrogen combine with one atom of oxygen to make one molecule of water. H_2O is the shortcut way to say water. A small number below the letter for an element is the number of atoms in a molecule of that element. In the shortcut way to say water (H_2O) there are two hydrogen atoms. A large number in front of the element shows the number of molecules. $2H_2O$ means 2 molecules of water. $2H_2O$ has four hydrogen atoms and 2 oxygen atoms.

When atoms or molecules combine to make new molecules, we call this a <u>chemical reaction</u>. The atoms or molecules that do the combining are called <u>reactants</u>. The new molecules that are made are called <u>products</u>. The formula

$$HCl + NaOH \rightarrow NaCl + H_2O$$

shows one way salt is made. HCl is hydrochloric acid. HCl is made of hydrogen (H) and chlorine (Cl). HCl combines with sodium hydroxide. Na is sodium. Hydroxide is a word for one oxygen atom and one hydrogen atom when they are part of a larger molecule. HCl and NaOH are the reactants in this chemical reaction. The products are NaCl and H_2O: salt and water. This formula shows that if you drop the right amount of NaOH in some HCl and stir it up, what you will get is salty water.

Formulas are the language chemists use to talk about the work they do. Once you get used to them, formulas are an easy, useful way to talk about chemical reactions.

16. The main idea of this passage is

_____(1) proteins are the largest molecules

_____(2) the world is made up of atoms

_____(3) molecules are often very large

_____(4) chemical formulas are the shorthand of chemistry

_____(5) atoms or molecules that combine are called reactants

17.   When water is formed,

_____(1)   two molecules of hydrogen combine with one molecule of oxygen

_____(2)   two molecules of oxygen combine with one molecule of hydrogen

_____(3)   two molecules of hydrogen combine with one molecule of sodium

_____(4)   two molecules of sodium combine with one molecule of hydrogen

_____(5)   two atoms of hydrogen combine with one atom of oxygen

18. $4H_2O$ means

_____(1)   four molecules of water

_____(2)   four atoms of water

_____(3)   four reactions of water

_____(4)   four molecules of salt

_____(5)   four atoms of salt

19.   Hydrochloric acid and sodium hydroxide combine to make

_____(1)   hydrogen acid

_____(2)   sodium acid

_____(3)   salty water

_____(4)   acid salts

_____(5)   hydrogen oxide

20.   After reading this passage, you can conclude that

_____(1)   chemical formulas usually represent reactions

_____(2)   chemical formulas represent only atoms

_____(3)   chemical formulas represent only molecules

_____(4)   chemical formulas make the chemists' work more difficult

_____(5)   chemical formulas represent only electrons

Answers start on page 104.

CHEMISTRY PASSAGE 5

> **KEY WORDS**
> **metal**—(noun) a shiny substance that can be melted and
>   that can carry heat and electricity
> **alloy**—(noun) a metal that is made by melting together two
>   or more different metals

There are some chemicals that we use every day. Metals are chemicals that are very important in our everyday lives. Cars, stoves, forks, keys and jewelry are only a few of the things that are made of metal. A metal is a substance that carries heat and electricity well. Metals can be hammered into sheets and they usually look shiny. Metals are important to us because of their hardness and strength and because we can work with them to make many different things.

Some metals are elements; others are compounds. Gold, silver, iron, tin, copper and lead are all metals that are elements. Mercury, which is a liquid metal, is also an element. These elements can be combined to make new metals that can do different things. These combinations of metals are called alloys. Alloys are sometimes more useful than the elements they are made from. The element iron, for example, is very strong. But iron will rust when it is exposed to water or air for a long time. When iron is combined with the right amounts of nickel and chromium, we get the alloy stainless steel. Stainless steel will not rust, crack or scratch. Stainless steel is much better than iron for making knives and other kitchen tools.

German silver is an alloy made from copper, zinc and nickel. This alloy is beautiful and shiny, but it costs less than gold or silver. German silver is an alloy that is good for making jewelry. Gold is a beautiful and rare element but is also very soft. When gold is combined with zinc and nickel, we get the alloy white gold. White gold is harder than gold and can be used in some cases where gold cannot be used.

Alloys are useful in many ways as you can see by the chart that follows. Chemistry shows us the way to combine the natural elements of the earth so that they will be more helpful.

ALLOY	METALS USED	USES
brass	copper, zinc	fireplace sets, cookware, ornaments
bronze	copper, tin	ancient tools, statues, guns
dentist's amalgam	copper, mercury	fillings for teeth
German silver	copper, zinc, nickel	jewelry
pewter	tin, antimony, copper, bismuth	early American utensils
solder	lead, tin	joining metals
stainless steel	iron, nickel, chromium	knives, kitchen utensils
white gold	gold, zinc, nickel	jewelry, watch cases

21.   A good title for this passage would be

_____(1)   Metals Carry Electricity

_____(2)   Some Metals Are Soft

_____(3)   Stainless Steel and Its Uses

_____(4)   Useful Alloys

_____(5)   Metals Carry Heat

22.   Alloys are

_____(1)   combinations of chemicals

_____(2)   combinations of metals

_____(3)   combinations of salts

_____(4)   combinations of gases

_____(5)   combinations of jewels

23.   One reason for the use of the alloy stainless steel is

_____(1)   that it is cheaper than iron

_____(2)   that it contains no iron

_____(3)   that it does not rust

_____(4)   that it is so soft

_____(5)   that it scratches easily

24.   White gold is made from

_____(1)   copper, zinc and nickel

_____(2)   copper, zinc and gold

_____(3)   zinc, nickel and iron

_____(4)   nickel, chromium and iron

_____(5)   gold, zinc and nickel

25.   One conclusion you can make after reading this passage is that

_____(1)   alloys are useful in many ways

_____(2)   alloys are only useful in industry

_____(3)   alloys are only useful in making jewelry

_____(4)   alloys are not very useful

_____(5)   alloys are always made from iron

Answers start on page 105.

CHEMISTRY PASSAGE 6

> ## KEY WORD
> **synthetic product**—(noun) something that doesn't exist naturally in the world, but is made by humans

Some of the things we use every day are found naturally on Earth. Iron, wood and cotton are all products of nature. As our knowledge of chemistry has grown, we have been able to make new chemicals that don't exist in nature. These man-made chemicals are called artificial or synthetic products.

Chemists have been very successful at making synthetic fabrics. Many of the clothes we wear today are made from synthetic fabrics. Polyester is a synthetic fabric. So are rayon and nylon. Rayon was first made in the early 1900s. Rayon is made from a natural chemical called cellulose. Cellulose is found everywhere in plants and animals. All living things are made up of cells. Cellulose is the

SOME USEFUL SYNTHETICS

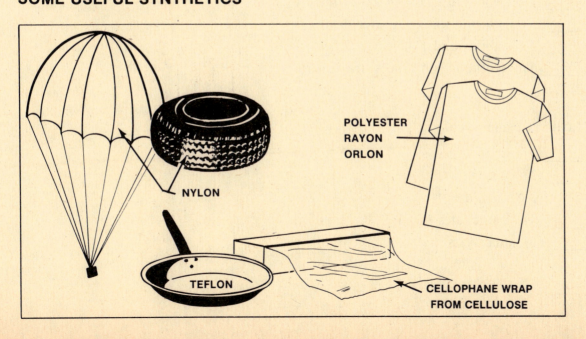

NYLON

POLYESTER
RAYON
ORLON

TEFLON

CELLOPHANE WRAP
FROM CELLULOSE

chemical that cell walls are made of. To make rayon, cellulose was first taken from spruce trees. Now rayon is made with cellulose from cotton seeds. Rayon cloth can be made to look like cotton, linen or wool. Paper and cellophane are other synthetic products made from cellulose.

Nylon is another synthetic fabric that is popular and useful. Nylon stockings can easily get runs in them, but actually nylon is a very strong material. Parachutes and car tires are made from nylon because it is so strong. Nylon is made from coal tar, a substance that comes from coal.

Orlon and Dacron are other synthetic fabrics. Orlon and rayon are sometimes combined with cotton to make a fabric that will wrinkle less than plain cotton.

Fabrics are not the only synthetic substances. Teflon and Bakelite used in cookware are synthetic. Fiberglass and all plastics are also synthetic. Many of the drugs used to cure diseases are synthetic. Without chemistry, synthetic products would not exist. Using our knowledge of chemistry to make synthetic products has made our lives easier and safer.

26. The main idea of this passage is about
   _____(1)   natural substances and their uses
   _____(2)   synthetic substances and their uses
   _____(3)   nylon stockings and coal tar
   _____(4)   fabrics and plastics
   _____(5)   synthetic substances are natural

27. Rayon is made from
   _____(1)   cellophane
   _____(2)   coal tar
   _____(3)   cellulose
   _____(4)   parachutes
   _____(5)   fiberglass

28. Synthetics are usually developed because they are

_____(1)   weaker than natural substances
_____(2)   less useful than natural substances
_____(3)   less popular than natural substances
_____(4)   more useful than natural substances
_____(5)   the same as natural substances

29. The product which is *not* synthetic is

_____(1)   rayon
_____(2)   fiberglass
_____(3)   nylon
_____(4)   paper
_____(5)   cotton

30. After reading this passage, you can conclude that

_____(1)   synthetic substances are always dangerous to life
_____(2)   synthetic substances make our lives easier and safer
_____(3)   synthetic substances do not have many uses
_____(4)   synthetic substances exist in nature
_____(5)   synthetic substances can be made without chemistry

Answers start on page 105.

ANSWERS AND EXPLANATIONS—CHEMISTRY

1. **(1)** is the best answer. Although all of the other ideas are in the passage, the main idea involves the study of matter.

2. **(3)** is the correct answer. None of the other choices is correct.

3. **(2)** is the correct answer. A compound is described in the passage as a combination of two or more elements.

4. **(4)** is the correct answer. Find this detail near the end of the passage.

5. **(5)** is the best answer. None of the other choices is correct, according to what is said in the passage.

6. **(4)** is the best answer. Although each of the other choices is mentioned in the passage, the main idea is to explain what particles are in the atom.

7. **(2)** is the correct answer. Choice (1) is outside the nucleus; none of the other choices name things in an atom. Orbits are paths, not particles.

8. **(1)** is the correct answer. The idea of atomic number is found in the fourth paragraph of the passage.

9. **(3)** is the correct answer. Find this detail at the beginning of the fifth paragraph of the passage.

10. **(4)** is the correct answer. None of the other choices give a correct conclusion, based on what is in the passage.

11. **(2)** is the best answer. Although each of the other choices is in the passage, the main idea is to explain how molecules are made.

12. **(3)** is the correct answer. Paragraphs three, four and five tell how many electrons are in each of the three shells.

13. **(1)** is the best answer. The examples of molecules given in the passage show that electrons may be shared or moved to form new molecules.

14. **(4)** is the correct answer. Find this detail in the paragraph about salt near the end of the passage.

15. **(2)** is the best answer. Electron shells do not have feelings, but they seem to "want" to be complete, or full.

16. **(4)** is the correct answer. Each of the other choices is given in the passage, but the entire passage is about how chemical formulas are written and used.

17. **(5)** is the correct answer. Find this detail in the second paragraph of the passage.

18. **(1)** is the correct answer. The example in the second paragraph of the passage shows that $2H_2O$ means two molecules of water. This would mean that $4H_4O$ would mean four molecules of water.

19. **(3)** is the correct answer. Find this detail in the third paragraph of the passage.

20. **(1)** is the best answer. Since combinations of chemicals are called reactions, that is what formulas usually represent.

21. **(4)** is the best answer. The passage gives all of the details listed in the other choices, but its main idea is the uses of alloys.

22. **(2)** is the correct answer. Find this detail in the second paragraph of the passage.

23. **(3)** is the best answer. None of the other choices is true, according to what is given in the passage.

24. **(5)** is the correct answer. Find this list of elements near the end of the third paragraph of the passage.

25. **(1)** is the best answer. None of the other choices is a conclusion that makes sense from reading the whole passage. Choices (2) and (3) give some of the uses for alloys. But in the whole passage alloys are said to be useful in *both* industry and jewelry.

26. **(2)** is the correct answer. Choices (3), (4) and (5) are in the passage, but they do not give the main idea. Choice (1) is not really discussed in the passage.

27. **(3)** is the correct answer. Find this detail in the second paragraph of the passage.

28. **(4)** is the best answer. All of the details given about the synthetic substances show that they are more useful in many ways than natural substances.

29. **(5)** is the correct answer. Choices (1), (2), (3) and (4) are all synthetic products listed as details in the passage. Cotton is listed as a natural product in the first paragraph.

30. **(2)** is the best answer. All of the details in the paragraph show that these products were developed to take the place of some natural products which were not as easy or safe to use.

UNIT IV: PHYSICS

Physics is the study of matter and energy. It includes such topics as light, sound, heat, magnetism, electricity and many other fields in which matter and energy work together.

Directions: Read each passage. As you read, think about the ideas, facts and examples given. Study any pictures or charts that go with the passages. The Key Words will give you an idea of what the passage is about. They are used in the passage along with other new words. Look up any word that is new in the Glossary at the end of the book. You will be able to figure out many new words as you read them in the passage.

After each passage, there are five questions for you to answer. Each question builds a reading skill. Make a check mark (✔) next to the BEST answer for each question.

The Answers and Explanations begin on page 124.

PHYSICS PASSAGE 1

> **KEY WORDS**
> **pitch**—(noun) high or low quality of sound
> **frequency**—(noun) the number of sound waves that go past you per unit of time

---

Have you ever changed a tire on a superhighway as a car sped by sounding its horn? The <u>pitch</u> of the horn seemed to change from higher to lower as the car passed by. Pitch is the high or low quality of sound. The same change in sound occurs in a train's whistle as the locomotive moves past you. This effect can even be heard on your television as a motorcycle speeds across the screen.

The change in pitch that you hear is called the Doppler effect. This change is due to the manner in which sound travels. Sound reaches our ears in the form of waves or a series of curves. It is almost like the ripples formed when you throw a pebble into a quiet pool of water.

The pitch of a sound is based on the number of waves that go past you per unit of time. This is known as frequency. When a sound has a high pitch, the frequency of the sound waves is greater than it is when a sound has a low pitch.

Look at the diagram that follows and pretend that you are the person standing near the car. In Figure 1, where the car is standing still, the horn has a pitch which we will call medium pitch.

As the car gets closer to you, the sound waves are pushed closer together. Figure 2 shows the greatest number of sound waves and the highest frequency. Therefore, the sound will have the highest pitch. The faster the car is moving toward you, the higher the pitch will be.

THE DOPPLER EFFECT

FIGURE 1

FIGURE 2

FIGURE 3

Finally, in Figure 3, after the car passes you, the waves move farther apart. The sound waves are fewer in number and the frequency is lower. Therefore, the pitch of the sound that reaches your ears is lower. The faster the car is moving away from you, the lower the pitch will be.

Although in reality the sound of the horn doesn't change, the Doppler effect explains the differences in what we hear.

1. The passage is mainly about

    _____(1) the Doppler effect
    _____(2) automobile speed
    _____(3) frequency of sound waves
    _____(4) changing pitch
    _____(5) superhighways

2. High or low pitch is based on

    _____(1) the frequency of light waves
    _____(2) the colors of the spectrum
    _____(3) the frequency of sound waves
    _____(4) an instrument to study sound
    _____(5) an instrument to study light

3. As the horn of an automobile coming toward you is blown, the pitch will

    _____(1) remain the same
    _____(2) get lower because the car is moving toward you
    _____(3) get higher because the car is moving toward you
    _____(4) get higher because the car is moving away from you
    _____(5) get lower because the car is slowing down

4. After an automobile moves past you, the sound of the horn will reach your ears

_____(1)   on clear days

_____(2)   at a high pitch

_____(3)   if it is raining

_____(4)   at a low pitch

_____(5)   at a medium pitch

5. From this passage you can conclude that the sound of a passing automobile horn will vary according to the automobile's

_____(1)   size

_____(2)   power

_____(3)   make

_____(4)   speed

_____(5)   color

Answers start on page 124.

PHYSICS PASSAGE 2

> ### KEY WORDS
> **momentum**—(noun) the motion that an object builds up as it moves
>
> **velocity**—(noun) speed; how fast an object is moving
>
> **friction**—(noun) the rubbing together of two objects which produces heat

Have you ever listened to a sportscaster describe a football game? Several times during the game the sportscaster may say, "The player's forward momentum carried him to a first down." What is the momentum that the player has in this case?

In physics, momentum is described as the motion that an object has built up as it moves. It is more than the speed itself. In fact, it is the product of the mass times the speed. The formula for momentum in physics is

$$Momentum = Mass \times Velocity$$

The mass of the object is its weight. Its <u>velocity</u> is its speed. If you could multiply the weight of the football player times the speed he was moving, you could measure his momentum. The player's speed is how fast he runs.

When measuring the momentum of moving objects, physicists usually must take into consideration that the momentum of the objects may be changing. Sometimes the <u>friction</u>, or drag, of the wind against the object affects its momentum. Friction also produces heat.

Momentum is important to measure in many different situations. The momentum of a spacecraft as it returns to Earth must be known so that a safe speed can be set. A safe speed would be a velocity that will bring the spacecraft back to Earth without burning the body of the craft in the earth's atmosphere. The body of the spacecraft would burn if its momentum was resisted too much by the earth's atmosphere. The larger the spacecraft, the lower its speed would have to be set in order to avoid burning.

6. What is the main idea of this passage?

_____(1) the passage is about momentum
_____(2) the author is writing about velocity
_____(3) mass is the topic of this selection
_____(4) the information concerns spacecraft
_____(5) motion is the main idea

7. One of the important considerations for scientists who are planning the return of a spacecraft into the earth's atmosphere is knowing its

    _____(1)   size
    _____(2)   mass
    _____(3)   speed
    _____(4)   velocity
    _____(5)   momentum

8. Momentum is the product of mass times

    _____(1)   size
    _____(2)   weight
    _____(3)   friction
    _____(4)   velocity
    _____(5)   force

9. Even if a football player is tripped as he runs down the field,

    _____(1)   his velocity may be measured
    _____(2)   his size could be increased
    _____(3)   his momentum might carry him forward
    _____(4)   his mass might be greater than his weight
    _____(5)   his speed could be increased

10. One conclusion that you could draw from this passage is that momentum would be important to measure in determining the

    _____(1)   speed of a baseball player rounding the bases
    _____(2)   strength needed by a car's brakes to stop it
    _____(3)   force of the wind in a fierce hurricane
    _____(4)   size of a spacecraft as it orbits the earth
    _____(5)   none of the above

Answers start on page 124.

PHYSICS PASSAGE 3

> **KEY WORDS**
>
> **astronomy**—(noun) the study of the stars, planets and all other bodies in space
>
> **heliocentric**—(adjective) sun-centered

At one time people who studied astronomy thought that the planets revolved around the earth. They thought that the sun also revolved around the earth. An Earth-centered system of planets made sense to earlier people. They could not imagine that some of the planets in the system were, in fact, larger than the earth. They also had no idea how far the planets were from the earth.

Eventually, thinking of the earth as the center of the universe caused some problems. The patterns for the trips that a planet made around the earth became hard for people to explain. By the time that the early astronomer Copernicus began to study the planets in the sixteenth century, people knew of 80 different patterns used to describe the movements of the planets around the earth. Copernicus did not believe that it was possible for the planets to move in so many different ways.

After a great deal of study he decided that the problem was thinking of Earth as the center of the system. The system of planets had to be based on some other body in the sky. It was logical to assume that that body is the sun. It was easy to observe how much larger the sun must be than the planets.

In 1542 Copernicus introduced his idea of a sun-centered system of planets. The system of planets then became a solar system or, as an astronomer would call it, a heliocentric system. This thinking solved many of the problems of an Earth-centered system. Astronomers could

THE SOLAR SYSTEM

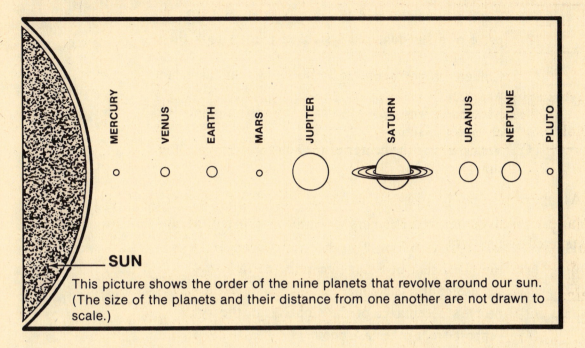

MERCURY VENUS EARTH MARS JUPITER SATURN URANUS NEPTUNE PLUTO

SUN

This picture shows the order of the nine planets that revolve around our sun. (The size of the planets and their distance from one another are not drawn to scale.)

now reduce the number of patterns observed to 34. Like most new ideas, however, people did not want to accept this one. It was logical, but not popular.

Copernicus had no way to prove that the planets revolved around the sun. Many astronomers finally accepted his idea that the two planets closest to the sun, Mercury and Venus, revolved around the sun. But most astronomers were not sure whether the other planets moved around the sun or not. Many still thought that none of the planets moved around the sun.

Therefore, it was left to Galileo, a later astronomer, to prove the truth of the Copernican theory. He was able to prove it through the use of the telescope. The telescope made it possible to see distant objects better. Galileo was the first to use the telescope in charting the course of the planets as they moved through the sky. One of the most important pieces of evidence came in Galileo's observation of Venus. Galileo's observations marked an important step forward in man's understanding of the solar system.

11. What is the main idea of this passage?

_____(1)   Copernicus discovered the solar system in 1542

_____(2)   proof of a sun-centered system of planets took time to obtain

_____(3)   Galileo did not want anyone to know that the earth was round

_____(4)   telescopes were always used by astronomers to observe the sun

_____(5)   Venus was at the center of the solar system until the sun grew

12. One of the most important factors in Galileo's proof of a sun-centered system was

_____(1)   the placement of Saturn near the earth

_____(2)   his use of the telescope

_____(3)   people's acceptance of the Copernican theory

_____(4)   support from other astronomers

_____(5)   a growing belief in the power of the sun

13. Based on the information in the passage, the Copernican theory must be

_____(1)   an attempt to describe the system of planets not including the sun

_____(2)   the idea that the earth is closer to the sun than Venus is

_____(3)   the thought that very few of the planets move in the sky

_____(4)   a description of the system of planets that Galileo did not believe

_____(5)   the theory that the sun is at the center of the system of planets

14. A heliocentric system is

_____(1)   an Earth-centered system

_____(2)   a system of 80 planets

_____(3)   the 34-planet system

_____(4)   a sun-centered system

_____(5)   the system made of helium

15.   One of the conclusions you can draw from this passage is that the people in the time of Copernicus

_____(1)   wanted to find out what Galileo would say later

_____(2)   thought that the 80-pattern system was a good one

_____(3)   were not ready to believe in a sun-centered system

_____(4)   liked the idea of a system centered around Venus

_____(5)   could not accept the theory then being used

Answers start on page 124.

PHYSICS PASSAGE 4

KEY WORDS
electricity—(noun) a form of energy
electron—(noun) a tiny, negatively charged particle found
    in an atom
repel—(verb) to push away
neutralize—(verb) to remove electric charge

Electricity is one of the basic forms of energy. It is carried by the electrons and protons in atoms. It has many uses. Electric lights, radios and televisions are all powered by electricity.

Here is a hair-raising experiment you can do yourself: Stand in front of a mirror and comb your hair while it is very dry. Comb it a lot, and use a very fine plastic comb. After a while you will see that your hair will not stay flat. It will begin to stand up on your head. Watch carefully as you pass the comb very slowly over your hair. Your hair will look like it is sticking to the comb. You can see this best by raising the comb very slowly above your head. Some hairs will follow the comb and stand straight up on your head. Why and how does this happen?

TRY THIS EXPERIMENT

Comb your hair many times.

Now pass the comb over your head. What happens?

What you have done is given an electric charge to your hair and to your comb. By rubbing your comb again and again against your hair you took tiny particles called electrons out of your hair and they are now on the comb. Electrons are some of the tiniest and lightest particles we can find in matter. They are much smaller than atoms. Every atom has one or more electrons. Every electron has what is called a negative electric charge. Normally, your hair has no electric charge. It is electrically neutral. When you take electrons away from it, you take some of the negative charge away. This is how your hair becomes positively charged. If you allow electrons to return to your hair, you are taking the charge away. It becomes neutral again. There are many electrons in the air so that after a while your hair is neutralized all by itself.

Why does your hair stand on your head when it has been combed a long time? Because each hair is now positively charged. All the hairs are trying to get away from each other. They repel each other because they all have the same positive charges. Same charges always repel each other. Why does it look like the hair is sticking to your comb? Because the comb has extra electrons. It is negatively charged. The negative charges on the comb pull on the positive charges on your hair. Opposite charges always attract each other.

There is something else you can try. Make sure your hair is very dry. Comb it in the dark, and comb only one spot for a long, long time. After a while you may see little flashes of light or sparks. What is happening? The electrons in the comb are attracted so strongly to your hair that they jump through the air and thus make little flashes or sparks.

16. This passage shows

    (1)   the best way to comb your hair

    (2)   the kind of comb you should use

    (3)   when objects are rubbed against each other electrons may go from one object to the other

    (4)   metals conduct electricity

    (5)   plastics do not conduct electricity

17. What can you say about electrons?

    (1)   every electron has a negative charge

    (2)   every electron has a positive charge

    (3)   some electrons are positive and others are negative

    (4)   every electron has at least two or three atoms inside it

    (5)   electrons attract each other

18. From this passage what do you think would happen if two negatively charged objects are brought close to each other?

    (1)   they would attract each other

    (2)   they would repel each other

    (3)   they would neutralize each other

    (4)   sparks would fly from one object to the other

    (5)   they would both become positively charged

19.   This section tells you that

_____(1)   there are two different kinds of charge, positive and
            negative
_____(2)   you can never neutralize a positive charge
_____(3)   you can never neutralize a negative charge
_____(4)   sparks can only happen in the dark
_____(5)   we do not know what causes lightning

20.   You can conclude from this passage that creating an electrical
      charge

_____(1)   can be done only by a trained physics student
_____(2)   cannot be done
_____(3)   can be done only when electrons are neutralized
_____(4)   can be very dangerous
_____(5)   can be done very simply with everyday objects

Answers start on page 125.

PHYSICS PASSAGE 5

KEY WORDS
gravity—(noun) the force that pulls objects toward the
      center of the earth
thrust—(noun) sudden power or force

Isaac Newton was a famous scientist. He discovered
three of the most important laws of physics. Newton's first
law was that a body at rest, or not moving, tends to stay at
rest. And a body in motion tends to stay in motion. Newton
was not writing about the human body, but was describing
any object at rest or in motion. He said that a body stays in

motion unless it is acted upon by a certain type of outside force.

Let us look at an example. When a car is moving, it will keep moving until the driver steps on the brake. Think of the brake as the outside force. When the car is stopped, it stays at rest until the driver steps on the gas again. The importance of Newton's first law is that it helps us to understand actions and reactions in the physical world.

Think of another example. What happens when you toss a ball? It travels through the air until gravity makes it hit the ground. Gravity is the outside force which changes the ball's motion. When the ball lands, it stays where it stops. It stays at rest until it is touched again.

Another example is an apple on a tree. While the apple is growing it hangs onto a limb of the tree from its stem. It is basically at rest. When it is ripe, it is heavy enough to fall. As it falls, it is in motion. Why does it stop? It hits the ground. The ground acts upon it as the outside force. Newton is said to have thought about apples falling to the ground as he worked on his laws of physics.

But how are these laws used? Well, think of an airplane. What gets it off the ground? If a body at rest tends to stay at rest, why does the plane take off? The plane's engine has enough thrust, power or force, to make it start moving and keep it going. When it slows down or stops, flaps on the wings are used to increase air friction. Also, the engines are reversed. These are the outside forces which overcome the plane's tendency to stay in motion.

Perhaps it sounds too simple when you think of the examples of the car, ball, apple and plane. But that is because you can easily see those things, and they seem natural. Without Newton's first law we would not have been able to design a machine like a plane. We would not even have been able to design a machine like a car. The designers of planes and cars have to consider many laws of physics in order to make their machines work.

21. The central idea in this passage has to do with

_____(1)   the laws of physics
_____(2)   a day with Newton
_____(3)   Newton's first law
_____(4)   most physics ideas
_____(5)   the motion of cars

22. Based on the information in the passage, what would happen if there was no ground to stop the fall of an apple?

_____(1)   it would stop because of its weight
_____(2)   the apple would expand as it fell
_____(3)   the apple would stay in the air
_____(4)   it would continue to fall
_____(5)   it would reverse its direction

23. What causes a ball to fall to the ground after it has been thrown?

_____(1)   speed
_____(2)   gravity
_____(3)   force
_____(4)   wind
_____(5)   thrust

24. What is the first part of Newton's first law?

_____(1)   a body in motion cannot stay in motion
_____(2)   bodies in motion will not come to rest
_____(3)   a body at rest tends to stay at rest
_____(4)   bodies at rest will move after a short time
_____(5)   a body at rest will not stay at rest

25. Based on this passage, you can conclude that a plane is built to fly

_____(1) even when it is acted on by outside forces
_____(2) only when there are no outside forces
_____(3) only when its flaps are being used
_____(4) only when its engines are reversed
_____(5) even when there are no outside forces

Answers start on page 125.

PHYSICS PASSAGE 6

> **KEY WORDS**
> **equation**—(noun) a statement using symbols which tells us that two things are equal
> **convert**—(verb) to change into something different

Over the years people have wondered about energy. Albert Einstein, the famous scientist, gave us one way to think about it. His theory tells us that every object contains energy. The amount of this energy depends on two things. First, it depends on the mass of the object. In loose terms, the mass of an object can be thought of as its weight. Also, the energy depends on the square of the speed of light, that is, the speed of light multiplied by itself. We use the letter C to symbolize the speed of light, so the square of the speed of light is C^2.

Does this sound confusing? It *is* complicated. But it is also helpful for everyone to have some idea about the relationship of solid matter, or mass, to energy. This is especially true when energy is such a problem.

Perhaps some day Einstein's work will lead us to a formula for changing many kinds of matter into energy. That's what his special <u>equation</u> is all about. The equation is $E = MC^2$, or energy equals mass times the speed of light squared. It tells us that mass can be <u>converted</u> to energy in theory. We know this to be true in simple ways—like the burning of coal. When coal is burned we get heat energy. We can also get heat energy from burning gas and oil. Einstein's formula describes the relationship between the coal, gas or oil matter and the heat energy produced.

People have known for years that burning matter will release heat energy. But now we are working on other ways of converting matter into energy. Nuclear reactions turn matter into energy. That is why nuclear power plants have been tried as energy producers. Of course, there are questions about the safety of nuclear power plants.

Questions of safety are just one type of question that is yet to be answered. Other questions have to do with what types of matter to try to convert to energy, how to achieve this conversion and how to harness the energy that is produced.

26. What is the topic of this passage?

     (1)   Einstein's ideas about matter
     (2)   turning matter into energy
     (3)   making fuel faster
     (4)   finding new fuel sources
     (5)   the end of burning fuels

27. What is Einstein's theory?

     (1) $E = MC^2$
     (2) $M + E = C^2$
     (3) $C + M = E^2$
     (4) $MC = E^2$
     (5) $CE = M^2$

28. What is done with the speed of light in the formula?

_____(1) it is multiplied times the energy and then squared

_____(2) it is added to the matter

_____(3) it is multiplied times itself and then times the matter

_____(4) it is divided by one-half and then added to the matter

_____(5) it is subtracted from the matter and then added to the energy

29. The author states that people have known for years that burning matter will

_____(1) create energy

_____(2) cause pollution

_____(3) release carbon

_____(4) improve it

_____(5) ruin it

30. One conclusion that could be drawn from this passage is that

_____(1) there is no chance of finding new sources of energy

_____(2) very few possibilities exist for finding more energy

_____(3) matter is always available for making more energy

_____(4) energy could be produced in new ways from matter

_____(5) no one knows what kind of matter has energy in it

Answers start on page 126.

ANSWERS AND EXPLANATIONS—PHYSICS

1. **(1)** is the best answer. Although (2), (3), (4) and (5) are mentioned, they are not the main topics of discussion.

2. **(3)** is the correct answer. The passage did not discuss (1) or (5), which concern light waves, or (2) the spectrum. Neither was there mention of the instrument used to study sound.

3. **(3)** is the correct answer. The sound waves are closer together, and are, therefore, more frequent, raising the pitch. Refer to Figure 2.

4. **(4)** is the best answer. Figure 3 illustrates that the sound of a horn reaches your ears at a low pitch when a car has passed you. (2) is incorrect. (1) and (3) may be true answers, but they are not discussed in the selection.

5. **(4)** is the best answer. The Doppler effect describes how a car's horn sounds different as the car moves. You could then conclude that the speed at which the car moves would affect the sound of the horn. (1), (2) and (3) *might* have something to do with how fast the car moves, but (4) is the most direct conclusion you might make from the reading.

6. **(1)** is the best answer. The other topics mentioned in answers (2) through (5) are included in the passage, but the passage is mainly about momentum. The other topics are described in their relationship to the idea of momentum.

7. **(5)** is the best answer. Scientists would want to know the spacecraft's momentum. Since momentum is the product of mass (weight) times velocity (speed), the other answers would be used to find the momentum.

8. **(3)** is the best answer. Momentum can keep an object moving even after it has been resisted by another force.

9. **(4)** is the correct answer. Remember that velocity can be thought of as speed.

10. **(2)** is the best answer. An engineer would want to know how far the car's momentum would carry it at different speeds in order to decide how strong the brakes must be. For instance, a tractor trailer moving at 60 mph would have more momentum than a sports car. The tractor trailer would need stronger brakes.

11. **(2)** is the best answer. Even though Copernicus showed that a sun-centered system was logical, it was hard to prove. Later,

Galileo used a telescope to chart the movement of Venus. Venus seemed to move around the sun. This was finally accepted as solid proof that the planets revolved around the sun.

12. **(2)** is the correct answer. (3) is not a good answer because most people still did not accept the Copernican theory. (4) is not a good answer because there is no suggestion in the passage that Galileo got any support for his ideas. (2) is correct because Galileo used the telescope to plot the movements of Venus.

13. **(5)** is the best answer. Copernicus was the first person to show that a sun-centered system made good sense. His work connected his name to the theory, or idea, that the sun was at the center of the system of planets including the earth.

14. **(4)** is the correct answer. Find this answer in the fourth paragraph. The author writes that the sun-centered system was called a solar system. Then the author writes that a solar system is a heliocentric system. So, a heliocentric system is a sun-centered system.

15. **(3)** is the best answer. (2) may be partially true, but people did not think about an "80-pattern system." They thought about a system with the earth at the center. They were not ready to accept the idea that the sun was at the center of the system.

16. **(3)** is the correct answer. (4) and (5) are both true but neither one is mentioned in the text.

17. **(1)** is the correct answer. (2) and (3) are completely false. (4) is false because electrons are inside atoms. (5) is false because electrons, being all negatively charged, repel each other.

18. **(2)** is the correct answer since same charges repel each other. (3) is wrong because same charges cannot neutralize each other. (4) is wrong because electrons jump from a negative object to a positive charge.

19. **(1)** is the correct answer. (4) is wrong because sparks happen all the time but it is easier to see them in the dark. (2), (3) and (5) are not true.

20. **(5)** is the correct answer. The passage tells a simple, safe way to make an electric charge.

21. **(3)** is the best answer. (1), the laws of physics, is mentioned generally, but the passage is mostly about Newton's first law. It is described in the first paragraph and discussed throughout the passage.

22. **(4)** is the correct answer. It would not stop because of its weight (1) because its weight would keep it in motion. It would not

reverse its direction (5) because "a body in motion tends to stay in motion unless acted upon by an outside force." It would continue to fall if the ground did not stop it.

23. (**2**) is the best answer. (3) is not specific enough. The force that causes the ball to fall is the force of gravity. That makes (2) the best answer.

24. (**3**) is the correct answer. The reader can find this statement in the first paragraph of the passage.

25. (**4**) is the correct answer. (2) and (5) are not possible. There is always some outside force. (1) and (3) are wrong since the passage mentions these as ways a plane is slowed down. (4) is the case when a plane flies, a car moves or a machine runs.

26. (**2**) is the best answer. (1) contains only a part of Einstein's ideas about matter and energy. The passage is about turning matter into energy.

27. (**1**) is the correct answer. The reader can find it in the third paragraph.

28. (**3**) is the correct answer. In the formula $E=MC^2$, the speed of light (C) is multiplied times itself or squared (C^2). Then it is multiplied by the matter to give the total amount of energy.

29. (**1**) is the best answer in this case. It is the information that is contained in the passage. People have not necessarily been aware of pollution for years (2), but they have burned wood and other fuels for thousands of years to keep warm.

30. (**4**) is the best answer. It is the answer that makes the most sense based on the information in the passage.

POST-TEST

Directions: The Post-Test gives a final look at your science skills. It is a good test of what you have learned. There are two types of questions on the Post-Test. Some questions follow a passage. The answers will come from your reading. Other questions, called "discrete items," stand alone. To answer these questions, you have to use your own experience or prior knowledge.

Place a check mark (✔) in the space next to the BEST answer. If you don't know an answer, you can guess. Take your time. There is no time limit. When you finish the Post-Test, check your answers in the Answers and Explanations section that follows. In the Answers and Explanations section, circle each correct answer. Then turn back to page 138 to fill in the Post-Test Skill Record.

Tides are created as the moon pulls on the earth. Water coming to the seashore creates a high tide. Water moving away from the shore is a low tide. Every day there are two high tides. When the earth is in line with both the sun and moon there are spring tides, which are very high tides. They occur when the moon is full or when there is no moon. When you can see a quarter moon, neap tides are formed. Neap tides are very low tides.

The highest part of a wave is the crest. The low part is called the trough. The measurement from crest to trough is considered the wave's height. The distance from one crest to the next is called a wavelength. If waves reach a height which exceeds one-sixth of their length, they form whitecaps and become unstable.

The pounding of waves wears down rocks and land formations. Sometimes waves deposit huge rocks and soil on the shore. Beaches and dunes are created by waves. Waves move sand in and out, forming inlets or cutting off bays from the ocean. This action of the waves has been very important in shaping the earth's surface.

1. The passage is about

    _____(1) tides and waves
    _____(2) streams and rivers
    _____(3) spring tides
    _____(4) full and quarter moons
    _____(5) measuring waves

2. A wave's height is the distance from

    _____(1) its wavelength to crest
    _____(2) its trough to wavelength
    _____(3) its whitecap to crest
    _____(4) its crest to trough
    _____(5) its head to its foot

3. A spring tide results when

    _____(1) there is a half moon
    _____(2) the waters of the ocean are warm
    _____(3) the moon is in the first or last quarter
    _____(4) it is a very warm spring day
    _____(5) there is a full moon or no moon at all

4. Whitecaps are formed as a result of

    _____(1) waves which flow north to south
    _____(2) currents which have mixed direction
    _____(3) tides which are very high
    _____(4) waves reaching a height one-sixth or more of their
             length
    _____(5) waves traveling at a speed of 20 to 40 miles per hour

5. From the passage you can conclude that waves

    _____(1) have little effect on the earth's surface
    _____(2) have a great effect on the earth's surface
    _____(3) are not important to scientists
    _____(4) are the most important scientific concern today
    _____(5) are regular and stick to one pattern

Children sometimes poison themselves. They can easily hurt themselves by swallowing common household products. Because they are curious, children reach for such things as bleach, cosmetics or paint thinner. They don't know enough to be afraid of what will happen if they drink or eat a poisonous substance. In fact, they don't know how to tell if something is poisonous.

There are several ways that parents can help prevent poisoning accidents. One way is to put a label on each container that has a poisonous substance and store it out of the child's reach. Children should then be taught not to touch containers with those labels. The phone number of the poison control center or other medical help should be kept close to the phone. Parents should know which products, such as activated charcoal or syrup of ipecac, counteract poison. Parents need to know what to do when an emergency occurs.

Even the most careful parents sometimes find that their children have swallowed a poisonous substance. If a child has taken poison, the parent's action must be fast. First, it is important to find out what the child has swallowed. Second, the poison control center, a doctor or other emergency medical aid should be called. Parents need to describe the poison and the child's symptoms and to ask for the procedures for treatment.

Poisoning can be prevented. But if it does occur, quick action can save a life or prevent serious injury.

6. The main idea of this passage is that poisoning

    _____(1) can be prevented or can be treated
    _____(2) cannot be prevented but can be treated
    _____(3) can be prevented but cannot be treated
    _____(4) cannot be prevented and cannot be treated
    _____(5) none of the above

7. The kind of poisoning that the author describes in this passage is poison that has been

_____(1)   seen
_____(2)   inhaled
_____(3)   touched
_____(4)   swallowed
_____(5)   purchased

8. According to the author's statements, poisoning may happen just because there are

_____(1)   three ways to poison yourself
_____(2)   many kinds of poisonous snakes
_____(3)   poisons in most household products
_____(4)   few rules for the prevention of poisoning
_____(5)   more poisons available than foods

9. Poisons may attract children because

_____(1)   they are brightly colored
_____(2)   children are curious
_____(3)   poisons taste good
_____(4)   pets eat them sometimes
_____(5)   parents can't control them

10. You should conclude from this passage that it is possible to treat cases of poisoning

_____(1)   if there is emergency medical help available
_____(2)   when the poison is very mild
_____(3)   even if medical help is not available
_____(4)   whenever the poison is known to be acid
_____(5)   under certain circumstances with a doctor

Reprinted by permission. © 1980 NEA, Inc.

11. From the cartoon, you can conclude that cells replace themselves

_____(1) slowly
_____(2) rapidly
_____(3) six times
_____(4) once
_____(5) twice

_____

12. Protoplasm is

_____(1) found only in plants
_____(2) found only in animals
_____(3) the living material of cells
_____(4) found in the air only
_____(5) one of the rare atoms

_____

13. An alloy is a

_____(1) good friend
_____(2) combination of metals
_____(3) silver coin
_____(4) pure form of metal
_____(5) pure element

_____

14.   Your weight is based upon

_____(1)   acceleration and velocity
_____(2)   sound and light waves
_____(3)   the force of gravity
_____(4)   electromagnetic forces
_____(5)   the Doppler effect

_____

15.   Pollution increased in the United States after a period known as the

_____(1)   industrious revolution
_____(2)   industrial revelation
_____(3)   industrious revolt
_____(4)   industrial revolution
_____(5)   industrial revolt

_____

16.   If water is present in the gasoline used in an automobile, it will

_____(1)   make it cheaper to run the car
_____(2)   block the gas line in cold weather
_____(3)   help the car run more efficiently
_____(4)   keep the gas line clean
_____(5)   help solve the energy problem

_____

17.   Using sandpaper to make wood smooth is an example of

_____(1)   genetics
_____(2)   magnetism
_____(3)   emergence
_____(4)   friction
_____(5)   pitch

_____

18.   Electricity is a moving stream of
_____(1)   clouds
_____(2)   static
_____(3)   generators
_____(4)   coal
_____(5)   electrons

_____

Plastics! That word was spoken with scorn in a popular movie during the Vietnam War era. Plastics came to stand for what people disliked about modern life. They seemed to be phony. They seemed to be cheap.

But they aren't anymore. Now plastics and the molds used to make plastics cost a lot. Plastics are made of a petroleum base. Petroleum is oil. Oil is very expensive.

Have plastics taken on a new image? Probably not. But they are in greater demand as the years go by. Almost every piece of heavy machinery built today has one or more critical parts made of plastic. Car owners are often surprised that their huge automobiles won't run because a small plastic part is broken.

Plastics are lightweight. Despite rising costs, plastic parts are still cheaper than metal parts. They are also surprisingly strong. And it is because plastics are light and strong that they are so useful.

Many plastics are today as strong as the glass or metal they replaced. They don't rust or scratch and they weigh much less. And, to top it off, some of the new plastics are heat resistant. The fact that they would melt under heat was a major drawback of early plastics. Many plastics today can be used under conditions that would have melted earlier types. Some can be used in ovens as casserole dishes. Others are used in spacecraft and airplanes. The bodies of some cars are made out of a type of plastic.

The desire to return to natural products may be with us for a long time. It may last even after most of our goods are made of plastic and other man-made products. But if plastics can give us better products at cheaper prices, they will be used. We will be better off for their use. Then we can save our natural products for making other goods. We will be using both the natural products and the plastics better.

19.   The thought that is most important to this passage is that

_____(1)   plastics cannot be used in place of metal
_____(2)   someday plastics will replace everything but wood
_____(3)   there are few problems with the use of plastics today
_____(4)   most people would prefer plastic objects to others
_____(5)   the day will come when plastics will be no longer used

20.   One of the important steps in the making of plastics has been

_____(1)   the development of heat resistant plastics
_____(2)   a discovery of a natural plastic
_____(3)   finding out what plastics are made of
_____(4)   using plastics inside ovens
_____(5)   molding plastics to any shape

21.   People don't seem to like plastics very much today because they think plastics are

_____(1)   useful
_____(2)   contemporary
_____(3)   artificial
_____(4)   expensive
_____(5)   natural

22.   One of the earlier criticisms of plastics was that they were cheap. Today plastics are expensive because they are

_____(1)   made with a petroleum base
_____(2)   used in place of steel
_____(3)   constructed with leather
_____(4)   baked in expensive molds
_____(5)   lined with copper strips

23. You could conclude from the author's comments on plastics that they will

_____(1) replace most wood products by the year 2000
_____(2) continue to cost too much to be useful
_____(3) provide us with a better standard of living
_____(4) prove to be too weak to be used under pressure
_____(5) prevent us from making full use of our steel

24. The universal blood donor is one who

_____(1) can give blood to any other group
_____(2) cannot give blood
_____(3) can only give blood to people with Type AB blood
_____(4) can only give to people with Type B blood
_____(5) can only give to people with Type A blood

25. The inner part of an atom is called the

_____(1) cell wall
_____(2) inner shell
_____(3) outer shell
_____(4) nucleus
_____(5) electron

ANSWERS AND EXPLANATIONS—POST-TEST

Main Idea   1.   **(1)** is the best answer. Although (3), (4) and (5) are mentioned, tides and waves are discussed throughout the passage.

Detail   2.   **(4)** is the correct answer. In the second paragraph the author states that the distance from the crest to the trough determines the height of a wave.

Cause-Effect   3.   **(5)** is the correct answer. A spring tide results when there is a full moon or no moon.

Cause-Effect   4.   **(4)** is the correct answer. When waves reach a height exceeding one-sixth of their length, whitecaps are the result.

Conclusion   5.   **(2)** is the best answer. The author explains that waves have been important in the shaping of the earth's surface.

Main Idea   6.   **(1)** is the correct answer. The entire selection deals with prevention and treatment of poisoning.

Detail   7.   **(4)** is the correct answer. In the first paragraph the author mentions poison that can be swallowed easily by children.

Cause-Effect   8.   **(3)** is the best answer. Children can be poisoned easily just because there are poisons in most household products.

Cause-Effect   9.   **(2)** is the best answer. Since children are curious, they are attracted to many household items including those containing poisonous substances.

Conclusion   10.   **(3)** is the best answer because the author gives the reader the impression that remedies can be given at home.

Conclusion   11.   **(2)** is the correct answer. The phrase "I've been six different people" is the clue to the reader that cells replace themselves rapidly.

Prior Knowledge   12.   **(3)** is the correct answer. Protoplasm is the living matter in all organisms.

Prior Knowledge   13.   **(2)** is the correct answer. An alloy is a man-made product or a combination of metals.

Prior Knowledge   14. **(3)** is the correct answer. The force of gravity is equal to 32 pounds per square inch. This force is exerted on all substances within the earth's atmosphere.

Prior Knowledge   15. **(4)** is the correct term. Pollution greatly increased as a result of expanded industry.

Prior Knowledge   16. **(2)** is the correct answer. Water blocks the gasoline line because it freezes in cold weather.

Prior Knowledge   17. **(4)** is the correct answer. Friction results from the contact of the sandpaper surface with the wood surface. As the two surfaces rub together, they each become smooth.

Prior Knowledge   18. **(5)** is the correct answer. Electrons are electrical charges.

Main Idea   19. **(3)** is the best answer. Plastics have become more popular and more practical through the years.

Detail   20. **(1)** is the best answer. At one time the tendency of plastic to melt under heat was a major problem. Today plastic is used for cookware, airplane parts and many other things that come into contact with heat.

Cause-Effect   21. **(3)** is the best answer. People still tend to think plastic is phony or artificial. Plastic has been thought of as a cheap substitute for the real thing.

Compare-Contrast   22. **(1)** is the correct answer. The author states that today, plastics are made from a petroleum or oil base. Oil is expensive.

Conclusion   23. **(3)** is the best answer. You can easily conclude that plastics will be used when they can give us a better product at a lower price than natural products. Natural products can be saved for goods which require them. With the right combination of plastic and natural products, we will have a better standard of living.

Prior Knowledge   24. **(1)** is the correct answer. The universal donor can give blood to individuals in any blood group.

Prior Knowledge   25. **(4)** is the correct answer. The nucleus is the innermost part of an atom.

POST-TEST ANSWER KEY

1. **(1)**	6. **(1)**	11. **(2)**	16. **(2)**	21. **(3)**
2. **(4)**	7. **(4)**	12. **(3)**	17. **(4)**	22. **(1)**
3. **(5)**	8. **(3)**	13. **(2)**	18. **(5)**	23. **(3)**
4. **(4)**	9. **(2)**	14. **(3)**	19. **(3)**	24. **(1)**
5. **(2)**	10. **(3)**	15. **(4)**	20. **(1)**	25. **(4)**

POST-TEST SKILL RECORD

Directions: Fill in the Post-Test Skill Record after you have taken the Post-Test and have checked your answers. The Skill Record will show your strengths in science reading skills and prior knowledge. Turn back to the Pre-Test Skill Record to compare your scores.

POST-TEST DATE: _____

Post-Test skills	Test Questions	Total Questions	Number Correct
• Finding the Main Idea	1,6,19	3	
• Recalling Details	2,7,20	3	
• Seeing Relationships			
Cause-Effect	3,4,8,9,21	5	
Compare-Contrast	22	1	
• Drawing Conclusions	5,10,11,23	4	
• Using Prior Knowledge	12,13,14,15, 16,17,18,24,25	9	
TOTAL		25		TEST SCORE

GLOSSARY

—A—

abdomen—(noun) the area of the body below the chest which holds the stomach and other organs used in digestion (Biology #1)

air pollution—(noun) smoke, gases and particles that make the air dirty (Earth Science #6)

alloy—(noun) a metal that is made by melting together two or more different metals (Chemistry #5)

antibody—(noun) a substance in the blood that attacks foreign proteins and that helps the body fight off infection and disease (Biology #9)

anxiety—(noun) worry or nervousness (Biology #4)

astronomer—(noun) a scientist who studies the stars and other planets (Earth Science #10; Physics #3)

astronomy—(noun) the study of the stars, planets and all other bodies in space (Physics #3)

atmosphere—(noun) the colorless, odorless gases that surround the earth (Earth Science #1)

atom—(noun) the smallest part that makes up matter (Chemistry #1, #2, #3; Physics #4)

atomic number—(noun) the number of protons in an atom (Chemistry #2)

atomic weight—(noun) the total weight of the protons, neutrons and electrons of an atom (Chemistry #2)

—B—

blockage—(noun) the condition of being blocked or plugged up (Biology #6)

breed—(verb) to produce or give birth to (Biology #1)

—C—

cell—(noun) the building block of living things (Biology #2, #5; Chemistry #6)

characteristic—(noun) a quality or feature that makes someone or something what it is or makes it different from other persons or things (Biology #5)

chemical formula—(noun) a short way of showing a chemical reaction; for example, $H_2 + O \rightarrow H_2O$ (Chemistry #4)

chemical reaction—(noun) atoms or molecules combining to make new molecules (Chemistry #4)

chlorophyll—(noun) the green substance in plants that makes photosynthesis possible (Biology #8)

chromosome—(noun) a rod-shaped body in an animal or plant cell nucleus that carries the hereditary information (Biology #5)

chromosphere—(noun) the sun's third layer of gas (Earth Science #8)

compound—(noun) two or more elements combined to form a new substance (Chemistry #1, #5)

convert—(verb) to change into something different (Physics #6)

core—(noun) the center of the sun (Earth Science #8)

corona—(noun) the sun's pale outer layer of gas (Earth Science #8)

crater—(noun) the opening at the top of a volcano where lava, smoke and steam come out (Earth Science #3)

cycle—(noun) a series of events that repeats itself in the same order (Biology #1, #8)

—D—

depend—(verb) to trust or rely on (Biology #2, #4)

depressant—(noun) a drug that slows down (depresses) body functions (Biology #4)

dominant gene—(noun) a gene that determines an inherited trait when combined with a recessive gene (Biology #5, #9)

drastic—(adjective) very strong or extreme (Biology #3)

—E—

earthquake—(noun) a shaking of the earth due to movements in the earth's crust (Earth Science #2)

electron—(noun) a tiny, negatively charged particle found in an atom; one of the three parts of an atom; electrons orbit the center of the atom (Chemistry #2, #3; Physics #4)

electron shell—(noun) one of the different layers in which electrons move around the nucleus of an atom (Chemistry #3)

element—(noun) matter, in its most basic form; for example, oxygen, hydrogen and carbon are elements (Chemistry #1, #3, #5)

eliminate—(verb) to get rid of (Biology #3)

energy—(noun) a kind of power or force such as electricity, heat or light (Biology #8; Physics #6)

equation—(noun) a statement using symbols; it tells us that two things are equal; for example, $E=MC^2$ (Physics #6)

erupt—(verb) to release or push something out suddenly and forcefully (Earth Science #3)

expand—(verb) to grow larger; to swell (Earth Science #8)

extinct—(adjective) no longer living on Earth (Biology #3)

—F—

formula—(noun) words or symbols that explain a rule or belief; for example, $H_2 + O \rightarrow H_2O$ is the formula for water (Chemistry #4) and Momentum = Mass x Velocity is the formula for momentum in physics (Physics #2)

fossil—(noun) the remains of a plant or animal that lived long ago (Biology #3)

frequency—(noun) the number of sound waves that go past you in a given unit of time (Physics #1)

friction—(noun) the rubbing together of two objects which produces heat (Physics #2, #5)

function—(noun) the normal job, role or work of a part of the body (Biology #4)

—G—

gene—(noun) information in the chromosomes about a particular trait, such as eye color, hair color or height (Biology #5)

genetics—(noun) the study of how traits are passed on (Biology #5)

genus—(noun) a division of a family of plants or animals (Biology #7)

geologist—(noun) a scientist who studies the earth (Earth Science #2)

gravity—(noun) the force that pulls objects toward the center of the earth (Physics #4, #5)

—H—

hallucinogen—(noun) a drug that makes the user see or feel things that aren't really there (Biology #4)

harness—(verb) to bring under control and use (Physics #6)

heliocentric—(adjective) sun-centered (Physics #3)

heredity—(noun) the means of passing on family traits (Biology #5, #9)

hydrosphere—(noun) all the water that is part of the earth (Earth Science #1)

—I—

ice age—(noun) a period of time when the earth's temperature drops and ice sheets cover much of the globe (Earth Science #4)

indicate—(verb) to show or point out (Biology #3)

interglacial—(noun) the time between ice ages (Earth Science #4)

—K—

kingdom—(noun) one of the two major groups of living things; the plant and animal kingdoms are these two major groups (Biology #7)

—L—

lava—(noun) hot melted rock that flows out of a volcano (Earth Science #3)

—M—

magma—(noun) hot melted rock inside a volcano (Earth Science #3)

matter—(noun) anything that has a size and weight (Chemistry #1, #2, #3; Physics #6)

metal—(noun) a shiny substance that can be melted and that can carry heat and electricity (Chemistry #5)

molecule—(noun) two or more atoms joined (Chemistry #3)

momentum—(noun) the motion that builds up as an object moves (Physics #2)

—N—

natural resource—(noun) a product of nature such as water, coal, trees and fish (Biology #1)

neutralize—(verb) to remove the electric charge from something (Physics #4)

neutron—(noun) one of the three parts of an atom; neutrons are found in the nucleus of the atom (Chemistry #2, #3)

non-renewable resource—(noun) a resource that cannot be replaced when used up; oil is a non-renewable resource (Earth Science #5)

nucleus—(noun) the central core of a cell or an atom; an atom nucleus is made up of protons and neutrons (Biology #5, Chemistry #2, #3)

—O—

occur—(verb) to happen or take place (Biology #3)

oil shale—(noun) a rock that turns into oil if it is buried beneath the earth for many years (Earth Science #5)

organ—(noun) a group of tissues that work together (Biology #2)

organism—(noun) a living plant or animal (Biology #2)

—P—

pace—(noun) a rate of speed (Biology #2)

paleontologist—(noun) a scientist who studies fossils (Biology #3)

particle—(noun) a very small piece of something (Earth Science #6, #10; Chemistry #2, #3; Physics #4)

passive solar heating—(noun) a way of heating buildings with sunlight, using no equipment except the building itself (Earth Science #7)

personality—(noun) all of a person's traits, habits and behavior (Biology #9)

photosphere—(noun) a layer of gas that surrounds the sun's core (Earth Science #8)

photosynthesis—(noun) the process by which a plant uses chlorophyll and sunlight to make food for itself (Biology #8)

phylum—(noun) a group of related plant or animal classes (Biology #7)

physical—(adjective) having to do with things found in nature (Physics #5)

pitch—(noun) the high or low quality of sound (Physics #1)

plate—(noun) one of the pieces that make up the earth's crust (Earth Science #2, #3)

plate tectonics—(noun) changes in the earth's crust that are caused by movement in the plates that make up the crust (Earth Science #2)

predict—(verb) to make a guess about what will happen (Earth Science #6)

preserve—(verb) to protect, save or keep (Biology #1)

procedure—(noun) a way of doing something (Biology #6)

product—(noun) the new molecules that are made in a chemical reaction (Chemistry #4); the number gotten by multiplying two other numbers together (Physics #2)

protein—(noun) one of the basic chemicals found in all living things (Biology #9)

proton—(noun) one of the three parts of an atom; protons are found in the nucleus of an atom (Chemistry #2, #3)

—R—

reactant—(noun) the atoms or molecules that combine and change in a chemical reaction (Chemistry #4)

recessive gene—(noun) a gene that produces an inherited trait only when combined with another recessive gene (Biology #5)

recognize—(verb) to see something clearly or to know that something exists (Biology #9)

renewable resource—(noun) a resource that can be replaced after it is used up; trees are a renewable resource (Earth Science #5)

repel—(verb) to push away; like electrical charges repel each other (Physics #4)

respiratory—(adjective) something that has to do with breathing (Biology #4)

restore—(verb) to return something to its original condition (Biology #1, #6)

Rh factor—(noun) a protein found in the blood of most people (Rh+) and not found in the blood of some people (Rh−); an inherited trait (Biology #9)

Richter scale—(noun) a scale for measuring how strong an earthquake is (Earth Science #2)

—S—

seismograph—(noun) a machine that measures how strong an earthquake is (Earth Science #2)

solar system—(noun) a star and the planets that orbit it (Earth Science #9, #10; Physics #3)

spawn—(verb) to lay eggs (fish, frogs and other water animals) (Biology #1)

specialize—(verb) to take on a particular job or purpose (Biology #2)

species—(noun) the most closely related group of plants or animals (Biology #5, #7)

stimulant—(noun) a drug that speeds up (stimulates) body functions (Biology #4)

suffocation—(noun) death caused by a lack of air (Biology #6)

symptom—(noun) a sign of some problem, illness or condition (Biology #6)

synthetic product—(noun) something that doesn't exist naturally in the world, but is made by humans (Chemistry #6)

system—(noun) a group of organs that work together (Biology #2)

—T—

theory—(noun) an idea that explains the reason for something (Biology #3; Physics #6)

thrust—(noun) sudden power or force (Biology #6; Physics #5)

tissue—(noun) a group of cells that look alike and do the same job; for example, muscle, fat and nerves are tissues (Biology #2)

trait—(noun) a physical characteristic that may or may not be passed from parent to child (Biology #5, #7)

transfusion—(noun) giving blood directly from one person to another (Biology #9)

—V—

velocity—(noun) speed; how fast an object is moving (Physics #2)

victim—(noun) a person who is hurt or killed by someone or something (Biology #6)

volcano—(noun) a deep opening in the earth's crust where melted rock from inside the earth flows out and cools, forming a mountain (Earth Science #3)

—W—

water pollution—(noun) waste from factories, sewage systems or other sources which makes the water dirty (Earth Science #6)